# Quilts a la Carte

## Pam Bono Designs, Inc.

Q Quilting is the food that fuels our creativity.

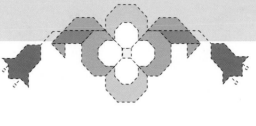

# Quilts a la Carte

**Published by**

**LEISURE ARTS**

LEISURE ARTS
P. O. Box 55595
Little Rock, AR 72215
www.leisurearts.com

**Produced by**

Pam Bono Designs, Inc.

P.O. Box 1049
Durango, CO 81302
www.pambonodesigns.com

## EDITORIAL STAFF

**Editor-in-Chief:**
Pam Bono

**Editorial Assistants**
Gigi Thompson and Cathie Childers

**Editors**
Gigi Thompson, Cathie Childers, Leah Schuster,
Robert Bono, and Faye Gooden

**Art Director and Book Design**
Pam Bono

**Graphic Illustrations**
Pam Bono

**Photographer For Pam Bono Designs**
Christopher Marona

**Photographer For Zelda Wisdom**
Shane Young

**Photo Stylists**
Pam Bono, Christopher Marona, Robert Bono and
Gigi Thompson

**Photo Stylists for Zelda Wisdom**
Carol Gardner and Shane Young

Made in the United States of America.

Softcover ISBN 1-57486-294-4

10 9 8 7 6 5 4 3 2

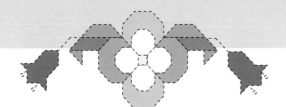

## Dedication:

I have always dedicated our books to special people in our lives. This book is dedicated to the loving animals that we have lost in the past three years who brought us unconditional love.

To the dog love of my life, Luciano Bono, the little white English Bulldog who loved music and sang opera. He was a tenor.

To our little "Raisin", a small English Bulldog lady with a huge heart and spirit. She lived a life and a half.

To our beautiful Old English Sheepdog, "Little Bear", the gentle soul, whom we lost in July to cancer.

To my little doe, "Webster" and her son "Jack." Our bond was a gift that is only given to someone who respects and understands the true meaning of wild and free.

## Credits

Designs by Pam and Robert Bono. "From The Earth" design by Mindy Kettner and Pam Bono.
Place mat pocket designs: Gigi Thompson.
Quilting by Faye Gooden and Julie Tebay.
Finishing by Suzanne Gamble of Durango Design Center, Gigi Thompson, and Julie Tebay.
Cake decoration and design by Laura Davis Baker.

## Special Thanks To:

Sandra Case and Jeff Curtis of Leisure Arts. It's great to have truly nice people like you to work with.

Nancy and Richard for allowing us to shoot in your exceptional home.

Nancy and Jim Burpee for giving us two days to shoot in your beautiful home. Thank you so much.

Celeste Gardner, owner of the Apple Orchard Inn in Durango, Colorado. Special thanks for giving us the creative freedom to shoot at your beautiful Bed and Breakfast.

Husqvarna Viking Sewing Machine Company for the loan of our Designer 1 machines.

RJR Fabrics for your supply of beautiful fabrics.

P & B Textiles for supplying us with your fabrics for projects in this book.

E. E. Schenck (Maywood Studio) for allowing us to create with your wonderful fabrics.

Our friends, Pat and John Nicholas who continually loan us their treasures for photography. Your friendship is appreciated and I spelled it right this time!

Carol Gardner, who made it possible for us to have the modeling sensation, Zelda (The Big "Z") in our book for everyone to enjoy.

# Table of Contents

For The Birds
Place Mat Set
Pages 24-27

The Bears &
The Bees
Tablecloth
Pages 12-15

Romance
Table
Runner
Pages 28-31

Old
Glory
Place Mat
Pages 16-17

The Cat's Meow
Place Mat
Pages 32-34

Pineapple
Passion
Place Mat
Pages 18-20

Northwoods
Tablecloths
and
Chair
Covers
Pages 35-44

Fanfare
Table Runner
and
Place Mats
Pages 20-23

Pinky Floyd
Place Mat
Pages 44-46

Tom
Place
Mat
Pages
46-48

Goose
Tracks
Table
Runner
and Place
Mats
Pages 73-77

Tea Party
Tablecloth,
Chair Covers
and
Accessories
Pages 48-55

Peppermint Ice
Cream
Tablecloth and
Place Mat
Pages 78-84

A Patchwork
Lunch For The
Quilting Bunch.
Six Traditional
Place Mat
Designs &
Napkins
Pages 56-66

Moonlight
Serenade
Table Runner
Pages 84-87

From The Earth
Tablecloth
Pages 66-69

Reap What
You Sew
Table Runner
Pages 88-92

Poinsettia
Table Runner
Pages 70-72

Bloom Appetit
Table Runner,
Place Mat
and
Accessories
Pages 93-96

5

# Learning Our Techniques

\*\*The techniques that are shown on the following pages are used throughout projects in the book. Please refer to these techniques frequently, and practice them with scraps.

## STRIP PIECING

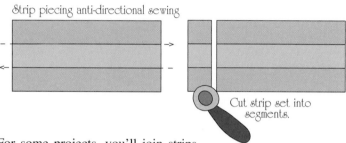

Strip piecing anti-directional sewing

Cut strip set into segments.

For some projects, you'll join strips of different fabrics to make what is called a strip set. Project directions not only show illustrations of each strip set, but specify how many strip sets to make, how many segments are to be cut from each strip set, and the specific size of each strip and segment. To sew a strip set, match each pair of strips with right sides facing. Stitch through both layers along one long edge. When sewing multiple strips in a set, practice "anti-directional" stitching to keep strips straight. As you add strips, sew each new seam in the *opposite direction* from the last one. This distributes tension evenly in both directions, and keeps your strip set from getting warped and wobbly.

## DIAGONAL CORNERS

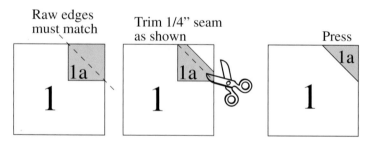

Raw edges must match

Trim 1/4" seam as shown

Press

This technique turns squares into sewn triangles. It is especially helpful if the corner triangle is very small, because it's easier to cut and handle a square than a small triangle. By sewing squares to squares, you don't have to guess where the seam allowance meets, which can be difficult with triangles. Project instructions give the size of the fabric pieces needed. These sizes given in the cutting instructions include seam allowance. The base triangle is either a square or rectangle, but the contrasting corner is <u>always</u> a square.

**1.** To make a diagonal corner, with right sides facing, match the small square to one corner of the base fabric. It is important that raw edges match perfectly and do not shift during sewing.

**2.** As a seam guide, you may wish to draw or press a diagonal line from corner to corner. For a quick solution to this time consuming technique, refer to our instructions on the following pages for The Angler 2.

**3.** Stitch the small square diagonally from corner to corner. Trim seam allowance as shown on the diagonal corner square only, leaving the base fabric untrimmed for stability and keeping the corner square. Press the diagonal corner square over as shown.

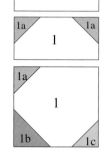

**4.** Many units in the projects have multiple diagonal corners or ends. When these are the same size, and cut from the same fabric, the identifying unit letter is the same. But, if the unit has multiple diagonal pieces that are different in size and/or color, the unit letters are different. These pieces are joined to the main unit in alphabetical order.

**5.** Many of our projects utilize diagonal corners on diagonal corners as shown below. In this case, diagonal corners are added in alphabetical order once again. First join diagonal corner, trim and press out; then add the second diagonal corner, trim and press out as shown.

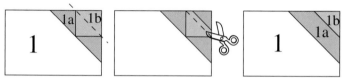

Diagonal corners on diagonal corners.
Join corners in alphabetical order.

**6.** Our designs also utilize diagonal corners on joined units such as strip sets. In this case, the joined units will have one unit number in the center of the unit as shown at right, with the diagonal corner having its own unit number.

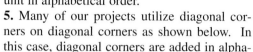

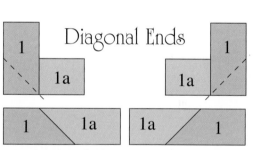

## Diagonal Ends

Diagonal End - Left Slant    Diagonal End - Right Slant

**1.** This method joins two rectangles on the diagonal and eliminates the difficulty of measuring and cutting a trapezoid. It is similar to the diagonal corner technique, but here you work with two rectangles. Our project instructions specify the size of each rectangle.

**2.** To sew diagonal ends, place rectangles perpendicular to each other with right sides facing, matching corners to be sewn.

**3.** Before you sew, mark or press the diagonal stitching line, and check the right side to see if the line is angled in the desired direction.

**4.** Position the rectangles under the needle, leading with the top edge. Sew a diagonal seam to the opposite edge.

**5.** Check the right side to see that the seam is angled correctly. Then press the seam and trim excess fabric from the seam allowance.

**6.** As shown, the direction of the seam makes a difference. Make mirror-image units with this in mind, or you can put different ends on the same strip.

This technique is wonderful for making *continuous* binding strips. Please note on illustration below, diagonal ends are made first; then diagonal corners may be added in alphabetical order.

**7.** Refer to Step 6 in *diagonal corner section.* Diagonal ends may be added to joined units in the same manner as shown below.

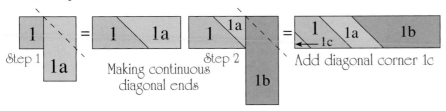

Making continuous diagonal ends          Add diagonal corner 1c

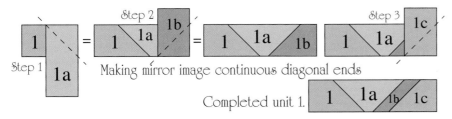

Making mirror image continuous diagonal ends

Completed unit 1.

Making mirror image combined unit diagonal ends.

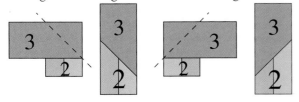

## TRIANGLE SQUARES

**1.** Many patchwork designs are made by joining two contrasting triangles to make a square. Many people use the grid method when dozens of triangles are required in a design. However, for the designs in this book we use a simple way to make one or more half square triangles. To do so, draw or press a diagonal line from corner to corner on the back of the lightest colored square.

**2.** As an extra tip, we have found that spraying the fabric with spray starch before cutting the squares to be used keeps them from distorting. A bit more fabric may be used; however, it is a quick and easy technique.

**3.** Place squares right sides together and stitch on the line. Trim the seam as shown and press.

**4.** The illustration at right shows how triangle-square units are marked in the book. A diagonal line is always shown, separating the two fabric colors. The unit number is always shown in the center of the square.

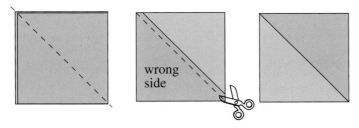

wrong side

## MACHINE PIECING

An accurate, consistent 1/4" seam allowance is essential for good piecing. If each seam varies by the tiniest bit, the difference multiplies greatly by the time the block is completed. Before you start a project, be sure your machine is in good working order and

that you can sew a precise 1/4" seam allowance. Refer to instructions and illustrations for use of The Angler 2 in this section to aid with accurate seams.

**1.** Set your sewing machine to 12-14 stitches per inch. Use 100%-cotton or cotton/polyester sewing thread.

**2.** Match pieces to be sewn with right sides facing. Sew each seam from cut edge to cut edge of the fabric piece. It is not necessary to backstitch, because most seams will be crossed and held by another seam.

## SEWING AN "X"

**1.** When triangles are pieced with other units, seams should cross in an "X" on the back. If the joining seam goes precisely through the center of the "X", the triangle will have a nice sharp point on the front.

## PRESS AND PIN

**1.** To make neat corners and points, seams must meet precisely. Pressing and pinning can help achieve matched seams.

**2.** To press, set your iron on cotton. Use an up-and-down motion, lifting the iron from spot to spot. Sliding the iron back and forth can push seams out of shape. First press the seam flat on the wrong side; then open the piece and press the right side.

**3.** Press patchwork seam allowance to one side, not open as in dressmaking. If possible, press toward the darker fabric to avoid seam allowance showing through light fabric. Press seam allowances in opposite directions from row to row. By offsetting seam allowances at each intersection, you reduce the bulk under the patchwork. This is more important than pressing seam allowances toward dark fabric.

**4.** Use pins to match seam lines. With right sides facing, align opposing seams, nesting seam allowances. On the top piece, push a pin through the seam line 1/4" from the edge. Then push the pin through the bottom seam and set it. Pin all matching seams; then stitch the joining seams, removing pins as you sew.

## EASING FULLNESS

**1.** Sometimes two units that should be the same size are slightly different. When joining such units, pin-match opposing seams. Sew the seam with the shorter piece on top. As you sew, the feed dogs ease the fullness on the bottom piece. This is called "sewing with a baggy bottom."

**2.** If units are too dissimilar to ease without puckering, check each one to see if the pieces were correctly cut and that the seams are 1/4" wide. Remake the unit that varies the most from the desired size.

## CHAIN PIECING

**1.** Chain piecing is an efficient way to sew many units in one operation, saving time and thread. Line up several units to be sewn. Sew the first unit as usual, but at the end of the seam do not backstitch, clip the thread, or lift the presser foot. Instead, feed the next unit right on the heels of the first. There will be a little twist of thread between each unit. Sew as many seams as you like on a chain. Keep the chain intact to carry to the ironing board and clip the threads as you press.

## Straight-Grain Binding

### Diagram 1

Cut two 3 1/2" wide strips for each place mat. Join them together as shown, using The Angler 2, or drawing a diagonal seam guide line.
Cut straight-grain binding. Bias is NOT necessary and is used mostly for curves. It makes
binding harder for beginners and wastes a lot of fabric for smaller projects.

Press under 1/4" on the long edge of the binding.

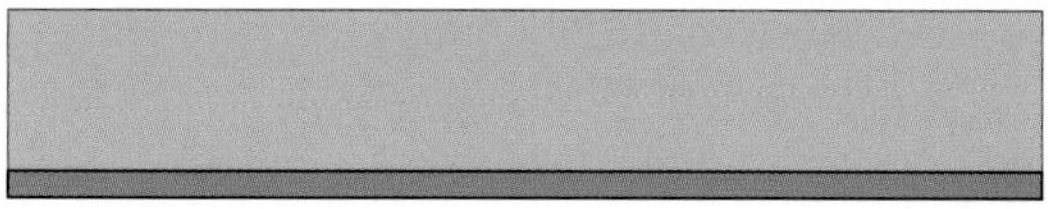

Matching right sides, and beginning at lower edge of place mat, pin unpressed edge of binding to place mat front, approximately 3" from end of place mat, (dot) leaving a 6" tail.
Continue pinning to within 1" of corner. Mark this point on binding. Use a 1" seam allowance and stitch to your mark. Backstitch at beginning of stitching and again when you reach your mark. Lift needle out of fabric and clip thread.

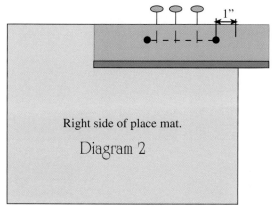

Right side of place mat.

### Diagram 2

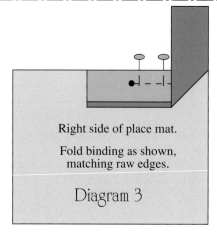

Right side of place mat.

Fold binding as shown, matching raw edges.

### Diagram 3

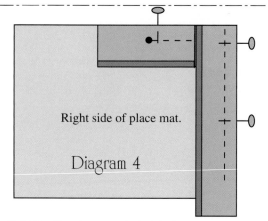

Right side of place mat.

### Diagram 4

Fold binding down, and pin binding to adjacent edge. Continue pinning to within 1" of next corner. Mark this point on binding. Continue this method, stitching around place mat. Reinforce your stitching at each marked point

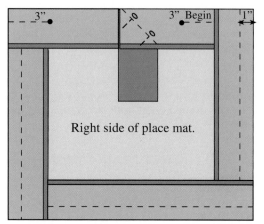

Right side of place mat.

### Diagram 5

1. End stitching about 3" from edge (dot), again leaving about a 6" tail. Reinforce stitching at both dots.
2. Fold left tail down at a 45° angle (perpendicular to top).
Bring other tail straight across on top of folded bottom tail. Draw a 45° line from top left to bottom right where they meet, and pin in place as shown.
3. As there is plenty of room that is unsewn between dot areas, pull the pinned binding out, and stitch the diagonal as illustrated on dashed 45° line. Trim seam 1/4" from stitching.
Complete sewing binding to place mat between dots, 1" from edge.

**This method does away with any lumpy overlaps, and is quick and easy!**

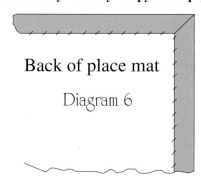

### Back of place mat

### Diagram 6

1. Trim the batting and backing even with the 1" seam allowance so that the wide binding is filled.
2. Fold the binding over the seam allowance to back. Blind stitch the folded edge of the binding to the backing fabric. Fold and miter into the binding at back corners.

 Robert invented the first Angler between our first and second books for Oxmoor House/Leisure Arts. He watched me drawing diagonal line seam guides that took forever! He said: "There has got to be a quicker way!" He found a quicker way. This little tool is now used by millions of quilters all over the world with results that cut piecing time in half, after a bit of practice. The instructions and illustrations are shown for the new upgrade, allowing you to make up to 7 3/4" squares. It can be purchased where ever sewing notions are sold.

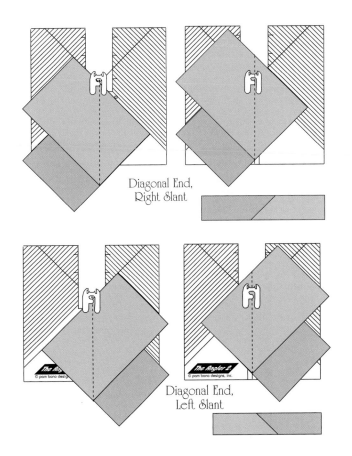

Diagonal End,
Right Slant

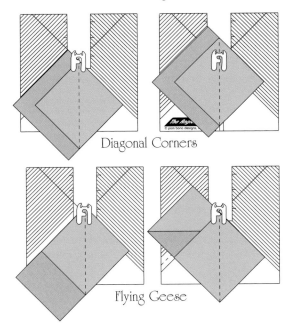

Diagonal Corners

Flying Geese

## DIAGONAL CORNERS & FLYING GEESE

**1.** Align diagonal corners with raw edges matching. Line fabric up so that right side of square is aligned with first 45° line on right as shown above, with the tip of the fabric under the needle. No seam guide lines will need to be drawn unless the square is larger than 7 3/4". As feed dogs pull the fabric through the machine, keep fabric aligned with the diagonal lines on the right until center line of The Angler 2 bottom is visible.

**2.** Keep the tip of the square on this line as the diagonal corner is fed through the machine. Trim seam as shown in our "quick piecing" technique section and press.

**3.** For Flying Geese, sew first diagonal corner. Trim seam and press; then join second diagonal corner. Trim seam and press. Overlap will give you an accurate 1/4" seam allowance.

## DIAGONAL ENDS

**1.** For both slants, prepare rectangles with raw edges matching. For right slant, align top rectangle with the first 45° line on right side of The Angler 2.

**2.** Bottom rectangle should align on first 45° left line as shown. As feed dogs pull fabric through machine, keep fabric aligned with the diagonal lines on the right until center line on The Angler 2 bottom is visible. Keep the top of the rectangle on this line as it is fed through the machine. Trim seam and press.

**3.** For left slant, line top rectangle up with the first 45° line on left side of The Angler 2 as shown. As rectangles are fed through the machine, keep top rectangle aligned with left diagonal lines on The Angler 2. This technique is great for joining binding strips.

Diagonal End,
Left Slant

## TRIANGLE-SQUARES, METHOD 2

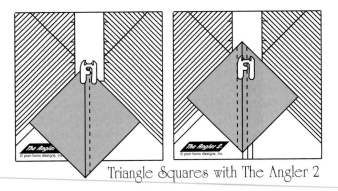

Triangle Squares with The Angler 2

Prepare squares with right sides together and raw edges matching. Line up the right side of the squares on line 1 on the right side of The Angler 2 as shown. Left side of square needs to be aligned with dashed diagonal line on The Angler 2. As feed dogs pull square through machine, keep top part of square aligned with the diagonal lines on the Angler 2 until left seam line is visible as shown. Keep point on this line until seam is sewn. Turn square around and repeat for other seam. Seams will be 1/4" from center as shown. Cut triangle-squares apart on center line and trim off tips and press.

## ACCURATE 1/4" SEAMS

Fabric is lined up on the computer generated 1/4" seam line on The Angler 2, and stitching is along center guide line. To take a full 1/4" seam, line fabric up on 1/4" seam line. If you want a "scant" 1/4" seam, line fabric up so that the seam guide line shows. We recommend a "scant" 1/4" seam as your seams end up being more accurate after they are pressed.

# Using Our Instructions....

The following points explain how the instructions in our book are organized. You will find that all projects are made easier if you read this section thoroughly and follow each tip.

• Yardages are based on 44-45" wide fabric, allowing for up to 4% shrinkage. 100% cotton fabric is recommended for the quilt top and backing. Wash, dry and press fabrics before cutting.

• At the beginning of each project, we tell you which techniques are used so you can practice them before beginning. Seam allowances *are included* in all stated measurements and cutting.

• The materials list provides you with yardage requirements for the project. We have included the exact number of inches needed to make the project, with yardages given to the nearest 1/8 yard. By doing this, we are giving you the option to purchase extra yardage if you feel you may need more.

• A color key accompanies each materials list, matching each fabric with the color-coded illustrations given with the project directions. We have made an effort to match the colors in the graphics to the actual fabric colors used in the project.

• Cutting instructions are given for each fabric, the first cut, indicated by a •, is usually a specific number of cross grain strips. The second cut, indicated by *, specifies how to cut those strips into smaller pieces, or "segments." The identification of each piece follows in parenthesis, consisting of the block letter and unit number that corresponds to the assembly diagram. For pieces used in more than one unit, several unit numbers are given.

• Organize all cut pieces in zip top bags, and label each bag with the appropriate unit numbers. We use masking tape on the bags to label them. This avoids confusion and keeps the pieces stored safely until they are needed. Arrange all fabric colors, in their individual bags with like fabrics together, making it easy to find a specific unit and fabric color.

• In order to conserve fabric, we have carefully calculated the number of units that can be cut from specified strips. In doing this, units may be cut in two or three different places in the cutting instructions, from a variety of strips. So that cut units may be organized efficiently, the units that appear in more than one strip are shown in red on the cutting list. This immediately tells you that there will be more of that specific unit. Additional cuts are not only shown in red, but the words "add to" are shown within the parenthesis so you may keep that zip top bag open, knowing in advance there will be more units to add.

• Large pieces such as sashing and borders are generally cut first to assure you have enough fabric. To reduce further waste of fabric, you may be instructed to cut some pieces from a first-cut strip, and then cut that strip down to a narrower width to cut additional pieces.

• Cutting instructions are given for the entire project as shown. To make one block, see information under "Making One Block."

• Cutting and piecing instructions are given in a logical step-by-step progression. Follow this order always to avoid having to rip out in some cases. Although there are many assembly graphics, we strongly suggest reading the written instructions along with looking at the graphics.

• Every project has one or more block designs. Instructions include block illustrations that show the fabric color, and the numbered units.

• Individual units are assembled first. Use one or more of the "quick piecing" techniques described on pages 6 and 7.

• Strip set illustrations show the size of the segments to be cut from that strip set. The illustration also designates how many strip sets are to be made, and the size of the strips. The strip set segments are then labeled as units within the block illustration. Keep strip set segments in their own labeled zip top bag.

• Each unit in the assembly diagram is numbered. The main part of the unit is indicated with a number only. A diagonal line represents a seam where a diagonal corner or end is attached. Each diagonal piece is numbered with the main unit number plus a letter (example: 1a).

• Many extra illustrations are given throughout the projects for assembly of unusual or multiple units for more clarity.

• Piecing instructions are given for making one block. Make the number of blocks stated in the project illustrations to complete the project as shown.

• Napkin folds are illustrated for napkins that require explanation as a part of the project.

## HOW TO MAKE ONE BLOCK

Cutting instructions are given for making the project as shown. There may be times that you want to make just one block for a project of your own design. All you have to do is count, or divide if preferred.

With each cutting list there is an illustration for the blocks (s). Unit numbers in the cutting list correspond with the units in the illustration. Count how many of each unit are in the block illustration. Instead of cutting the number shown on the cutting list, cut the number you need for one block. Should you wish to make two or more blocks, multiply the number of units X the number of blocks you wish to make.

## LIST OF SUGGESTED SUPPLIES TO START

**1.** Rotary cutter: There are several different types of rotary cutters on the market. They are available in different shapes and sizes. Choose the one that is the most comfortable in your hand. Remember, the larger the blade, the longer it will last. Also purchase replacement blades.
**2.** Cutting mat: The size of the mat is based of course, on the size of your cutting area. We use the 23" x 35" mat.
**3.** Acrylic rulers: We use several sizes. The favorites are: 8" x 24", 6" x 18", and the most used is the 3 1/2" x 12".
**4.** Sewing thread. Use a good quality cotton or cotton/poly thread.

**5.** Pins and pincushion. We especially like the long, thin, fine pins for quilting.

**6.** Seam ripper. We all use them frequently. We call them the "Un-sewers"!

**7.** Scissors. Here again, we use two or three different sizes to do different jobs.

**8.** Iron and ironing board. We use June Tailor's pressing mats next to our sewing machines for pressing smaller pieces.

**9.** Zip top bags, masking tape, and of course, The Angler 2!

**10.** If you are going to do the appliqués by machine, you will need good marking pens, stabilizer and a supply of machine embroidery needles, as they should be changed every 8 hours of sewing.

## APPLIQUE TECHNIQUES

We have used Steam-A-Seam 2 for every appliqué project in the book. We do not recommend it for large quilts, but it is an excellent product for smaller projects.

The large pattern sheet contains all of the appliqué designs. We have used an "Appliqué by number" system. Dashed lines within the designs show areas that fit behind another piece. Place each piece on background fabric in numerical order after the piece is cut. If you have an appliqué pressing sheet, we highly suggest using it as you will not get unwanted glue on your iron. We use an older steam iron when we do a lot of appliqué for this reason.

In the materials list, and the cutting list, specific sizes are given for the appliqué fabrics to be used. We have drawn the pattern pieces out and tested the sizes given so that there is plenty of fabric allowed.

When cutting the fabric, cut a piece of Steam-A-Seam 2 the same size. Please follow the instructions below as we have found this method to be quicker, easier, and more accurate.

**1.** Draw your appliqué designs on the unprinted side of the Steam-A-Seam 2 paper. Draw the pattern pieces close to each other, but allow enough room to cut easily.

**2.** Peel the drawn pattern side of the paper away from the fusible material, and place the fabric, right side facing up behind the drawn pattern sheet.

**3.** Place the drawn side of the paper and the fabric directly on top of the fusible material. The blue, printed side of the paper will still be attached to the back of the fusible material. Press the layers together with a hot steam iron, sandwiching the fabric.

**4.** Cut out the appliqués on your drawn lines. When all pieces have been cut for the design, peel the blue printed paper from the back of the Steam-A-Seam 2. You are now ready to press your cut pieces in place on the background specified in the project instructions in numerical order.

**5.** Please note that specific instructions are given in each appliqué project.

We used two methods of sewing the appliqués. Satin stitch was used for some; however we liked the look of the blanket stitch, especially on our cover design, "From The Earth." We used Robison Anton rayon thread for the appliqués.

Put a good press on, tear-a-way stabilizer behind your appliqués to keep them smooth.

## REVERSIBLE NAPKINS

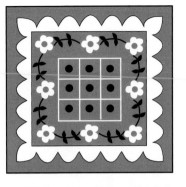

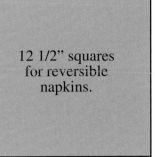

12 1/2" squares for reversible napkins.

Place right sides together and stitch. Leave opening to turn.

To finish, turn right side out and press. Place a small piece of Steam-A-Seam 2 (with paper removed from both sides) in the opening, close to the edge. We cut the piece the length of the opening and 1/4" wide. Press opening closed. This is a nice little trick that is quick and easy and eliminates hand stitching. It will stay together forever!!!

---

\* Please note that ⟵⟶ on any unit, indicates the longest side of the unit. We show this when difference of measurement (length and width) is only 1/8".

---

# The Bears & The Bees

Finished tablecloth size: 64" square. Quick pieced.
Techniques used: diagonal corners, and triangle-squares.

## MATERIALS

| | | | |
|---|---|---|---|
| ☐ | Fabric I  (white with yellow print)) | Need 57 1/2" | 1 3/4 yards |
| ☐ | Fabric II  (medium green print) | Need 40 1/4" | 1 1/4 yards |
| ☐ | Fabric III  (honey tan check) | Need 23" | 3/4 yard |
| ☐ | Fabric IV  dark brown print) | Need 14 3/8" | 1/2 yard |
| ☐ | Fabric V  (light honey tan print) | Need 6" | 1/4 yard |
| ☐ | Fabric VI  (medium honey tan print) | Need 8 1/4" | 3/8 yard |
| ☐ | Fabric VII  (solid black) | Need 27 7/8" | 1 yard |
| ☐ | Fabric VIII  (gray metallic silver print) | Need 3 5/8" | 1/4 yard |
| ☐ | Fabric IX  (bright yellow print) | Need 3" | 1/8 yard |
| | Backing | | 4 yards |

---

## Dorothy's Ranch Biscuits

### Ingredients:
2 cups flour
1/4 cup shortening
3 tsp. baking powder
1 tsp. salt
2/3 cup milk or buttermilk

### Instructions:

Mix flour, baking powder and salt together. Cut shortening into flour mixture. Add milk to form the dough, being careful not to over mix. Roll into a ball and roll out on floured cutting board so that dough is about 1/2" thick.

Using a biscuit cutter, cut the biscuits.

Pre heat oven to 450˚. Bake 10-12 minutes, and serve with honey.

All "Q" units in cutting instructions stand for tablecloth top. These are units that are not incorporated into the specific blocks, but are on the tablecloth top.

Cutting instructions shown in red indicate the quantity of units are combined and cut in two or more different places to conserve fabric.

# CUTTING

**From Fabric I, cut: (white with yellow print)**
- One 8 7/8" x 42" strip. From this, cut:
  * Two - 8 7/8" squares (triangle-square Q11)
  * Three - 6 1/2" x 8 1/2" (Q8)
- Four 6 1/2" x 42" strips. From these, cut:
  * Five - 6 1/2" x 8 1/2" (add to Q8)
  * Four - 6 1/2" squares (Q9)
  * Eight - 4 1/2" x 6 1/2" (Q6)
  * Eight - 2 1/2" x 6 1/2" (Q10)
  * Eighteen - 2 7/8" squares (B2 triangle-squares)
- Four 2 7/8" x 42" strips. From these, cut
  * Forty-six - 2 7/8" squares (add to B2 )
  * Eight - 2 3/4" x 3" (A2)
  * Eight - 1 1/4" x 2 1/2" (A6)

- Three 2 1/2" x 42" strips. From these, cut:
  * Thirty-two - 2 1/2" squares (B3)
  * Eight - 2" x 2 1/2" (A4)
- Two 1 1/4" x 42" strips. From these, cut:
  * Forty-eight - 1 1/4" squares (A5a, A9a, A11a)
- One 1 1/8" x 42" strip. From this, cut:
  * Twenty-four - 1 1/8" squares (A1b, A3a)

**From Fabric II, cut: (medium green print)**
- One 11 1/2" x 42" strip. From this, cut:
  * One - 11 1/2" square (Q1)
  * Four- 5 1/2" squares (D11) Cut in half diagonally. Stack this cut.
  * Two - 8 7/8" squares (Q11 triangle-squares)
- From scrap, cut:
  * Sixteen - 1 1/2" squares (C11b, D9b) Stack this cut.
- One 7 1/8" x 42" strip. From this, cut:

* Four - 7 1/8" squares (D12) cut in half diagonally
* Eight - 1 1/4" x 3" (C3, C9) Stack this cut.
- From scrap, cut:
   * Sixteen - 1 3/8" squares (C2a, D2a) Stack this cut.
   * Sixteen - 1" squares (C2b, D2b) Stack this cut.
- One 6 1/2" x 42" strip. From this, cut:
   * Eight - 4 1/2" x 6 1/2" (Q7)
   * Sixteen - 1 1/4" squares (C11a, D9a)
- Three 3 5/8" x 42 1/8" strips. From these, cut:
   * Eight - 3 5/8" x 4 5/8" (C12)
   * Eight - 3 5/8" x 3 7/8" (D10)
   * Eight - 2 5/8" x 3 5/8" (C10)
   * Eight - 1 7/8" x 3 5/8" (D8)
   * Twenty-four - 1 3/4" squares (C8a, C11c, D7a, D9c) Stack this cut
- Two 2 1/8" x 42" strips. From these, cut:
   * Eight - 2 1/8" x 8 1/2" (C13)
   * Eight - 1 3/4" squares (add to 1 3/4" sq. above)

### From Fabric III, cut: (honey tan check)
- Four 4 1/2" x 42" strips. From these, cut:
   * Thirty-two - 4 1/2" squares (B1)
- Four 1 1/4" x 42" strips. From these, cut:
   * Two - 1 1/4" x 34 1/2" (Q3)
   * Two - 1 1/4" x 33" (Q2)

### From Fabric IV, cut: (dark brown print)
- Five 2 7/8" x 42" strips. From these, cut:
   * Sixty-four - 2 7/8" squares (B2 triangles)
   * Four - 1" x 2 1/2" (A8)
   * Four - 2 1/2" x 2 3/4" (A10)

### From Fabric V, cut: (light honey tan print)
- Two 2 1/2" x 42" strip. From this, cut:
   * Four - 2 1/2" x 8 1/2" (A3)
   * Eight - 2 1/2" x 5" (A9)
   * Four - 2" x 2 1/2" (A7)
- One 1" x 42" strip. From this, cut:
   * Eight - 1" squares (A8a)

### From Fabric VI, cut: (medium honey tan print)
- One 3" x 42" strip. From this, cut:
   * Four - 3" x 7 1/8" (A1)
- One 2 3/4" x 42" strip. From this, cut:
   * Eight - 2 3/4" x 5" (A11)
- One 2 1/2" x 42" strip. From this, cut:
   * Four - 2 1/2" x 10" (A5)

### From Fabric VII, cut: (solid black)
- One 3" x 42" strip. From this, cut:
   * Sixteen - 1 3/4" x 3" (C4, C8, D3, D7)
   * Eight - 1 3/8" x 3" (C6, D5)
- One 1 3/8" x 42" strip. From this, cut:
   * Sixteen - 1 3/8" x 1 7/8" (C2, D2)
- Seven 2 1/2" x 42" strips for straight-grain binding.
- Four 1 1/2" x 42" strips. From these, cut:
   * Two - 1 1/2" x 36 1/2" (Q5)
   * Two - 1 1/2" x 34 1/2" (Q4)

### From Fabric VIII, cut: (gray metallic silver print)
- One 3 5/8" x 42" strip. From this, cut:
   * Sixteen - 2 1/4" x 3 5/8" (C11, D9)
   * Sixteen - 1" squares (C4a, D3a)

### From Fabric IX, cut: (bright yellow print)
- One 3" x 42" strip. From this, cut:

* Sixteen - 1 3/8" x 3" (C5, C7, D4, D6)
* Eight - 1 1/4" X 1 7/8" (C1, D1)

# TRIANGLE-SQUARES FOR THIS PROJECT.

Use the following method for triangle-squares in this project. To make them with The Angler 2, refer to page 9.

**1.** If you are not using The Angler 2, draw a diagonal line from corner to corner on the wrong side of the lightest fabric. Place this fabric right sides together with the other triangle-square fabric. If they are large squares, you may want to pin them so that raw edges match and stay together. Stitch 1/4" on opposite sides of the center line. Cut the triangle-square on the drawn center line. This method will yield two triangle-squares. Press open.

# ASSEMBLY

### Making Block A

**1.** Use diagonal corner technique to make two each of blocks 9 and 11. Make one each of units 1, 3, 5, and 8.

**2.** To assemble the block, begin by joining Unit 2 to opposite sides of Unit 1. Join Unit 4 to opposite sides of Unit 3. Join Unit 6 to opposite sides of Unit 5 as shown. Referring to illustration at right,

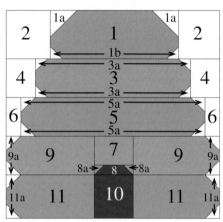

Block A. Make 4. Finishes to: 11 1/4" x 11 1/2"

join these three horizontal rows together.

**3.** Join units 7 and 8; then add Unit 9 to opposite sides of the 7-8 combined units.

**4.** Join Unit 11 to opposite sides of Unit 10 as shown. Join the 7-9 horizontal row to the top of the 10-11 combined unit row, matching door seams. Add these two rows to the bottom of the hive to complete the block. Make 4.

### Making Bear Paw Block B

**1.** Refer to instructions for making triangle-squares, and make 128 Unit 2 triangle-squares from fabrics I and III.

**2.** Refer to illustration at right for proper positioning of the bear paw units. Join two of Unit 2 together for the top of the paw; then join two together for the side of the paw as shown.

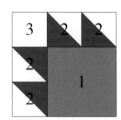

Block B. Make 32 Finishes to: 6 1/2" square

**3.** Join the top joined Unit 2's to top of Unit 1. Join Unit 3 to top of joined Unit 2's for side of paw. Join these combined units to left side of paw as shown, matching seams to complete the block.

### Making Bee Block C

**1.** Use diagonal corner technique to make two each of mirror image units 2, and 11. Make one of units 4 and 8.

**2.** To assemble the block, join units 3, 2, 4, 5, 6, 7, 8, and 9 in a vertical row as shown on page 15. Refer frequently to illustration for correct placement of mirror image Unit 11. Make another vertical row by joining units 10, mirror image Unit 11, and Unit 12. Make two of these rows as shown on Block C diagram.

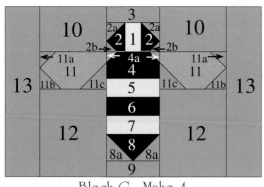

Block C. Make 4.
Finishes to: 8 1/2" x 12 1/2"

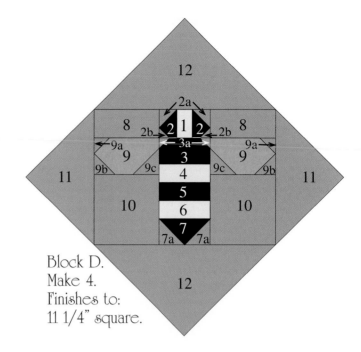

Block D.
Make 4.
Finishes to:
11 1/4" square.

**3.** Join the 10-12 rows to opposite sides of the bee center row, matching Unit 4a and Unit 11 seams. Join Unit 13 to opposite sides of the bee to complete the block.

### Making Bee Block D

**1.** Use diagonal corner technique to make two each of units 2, and mirror image Unit 9. Make one of units 3 and 7.

**2.** To assemble the block, join units 2, 3, 4, 5, 6, and 7 in a vertical row as shown. Refer to block illustration for correct placement of mirror image Unit 9. Make another vertical row by joining units 8, mirror image Unit 9, and Unit 10. Make two of these rows as shown.

**3.** Join the 8-10 rows to opposite sides of the bee center row, matching Unit 3a and Unit 9 seams. Join triangle Unit 11 to opposite short sides of bee; then add Unit 12 triangles to top and bottom to complete the block.

### Tablecloth Assembly.

**1.** Refer to diagram below and begin by joining Block A to opposite sides of Unit Q1. Join Block D to opposite sides of two remaining Block A's as shown, making certain that bee's are going in the right direction. They should all be facing towards the center. Join the three large rows together.

**2.** For center border, join Unit Q2 to top and bottom of center section; then add Unit Q3 to opposite sides. Join Unit Q4 to top and bottom; then add Unit Q5 to sides as shown.

**3.** For corner sections, join Unit Q10 and Block B. Make two. Join Unit 11 to one of the combined Unit Q10-Block B's, checking the diagram for correct placement. Join Unit Q9 to remaining combined Q10-Block B combination, again checking drawing to make certain that it is placed correctly.

**4.** Join the two combined sections together to complete the corner. Make 4 corners and set aside.

**5.** For the bee sections, join Unit Q6, Block B and Unit Q7 together in a vertical row. Make eight rows, checking illustration frequently as Block B will mirror image.

**6.** Join two Block B's together as shown. Make four; then join to top of Block C. Join Unit Q8 and Block B together as shown. Make eight with Block B mirror imaged for four. Refer to diagram and join the combined Q6-Block B-Q7 rows to opposite sides of the bee. Join the combined Q8-Block B rows to opposite sides of other combined units. Make four.

**7.** Join two of the bee sections to top and bottom of center section. Join the corners to opposite ends of the two remaining bee sections; then join to sides of tablecloth.

**8.** Faye quilted charming butterflies swirling around the bear paw blocks, and quilted large swirls in the center bee blocks.

**9.** Make approximately 275" of straight-grain french fold binding and bind the tablecloth.

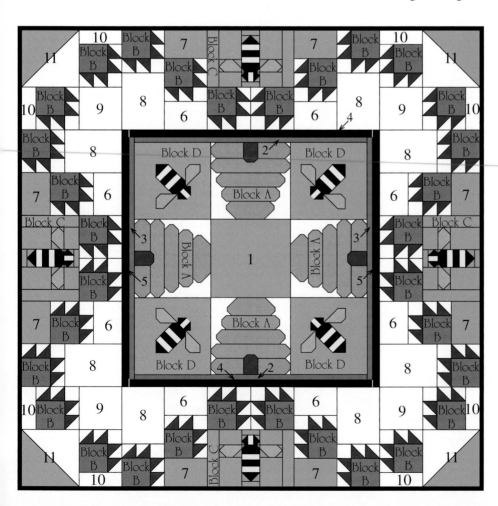

# Old Glory

## 12 Minute Pistachio Dream Dessert

### Ingredients
2 small packages of Pistachio Instant Pudding.
4 cups of milk
1 Angel food cake
1 - 8 oz. container of Cool Whip

### Instructions
Break up the angel food cake into 1"-1 1/2" cubes and place in a 9" x 13" x 2" pyrex casserole. Make pudding according to package instructions, and pour over cake evenly, allowing it to drip down to bottom of casserole. Top with Cool Whip. Enjoy this great, refreshing dessert!

NAPKIN

## MATERIALS

Flag place mat finishes to: 14" x 18". Pieced.

| | | | |
|---|---|---|---|
| ☐ | Fabric I (white on white print) | Need 7 1/4" | 1/4 yard |
| ▨ | Fabric II (red textured print) | Need 2 3/4" | 1/8 yard |
| ▨ | Fabric III (navy & white star print) | Need 12 1/2" | 1/2 yard |
| ▨ | Fabric IV (medium blue check) | Need 7" | 1/4 yard |
| | Backing and batting | Need 14 1/2" x 18 1/2" | |

## CUTTING FOR ONE PLACE MAT

 **From Fabric I, cut: (white on white print)**
• One 7 1/4" x 42" strip. From this, cut:
    * Two - 7 1/4" squares (pocket & pocket facing)
    * One - 2 3/4" x 18" (7)
    * One - 2" x 18" (6)
    * Two - 2" x 11 1/4" (3)

**From Fabric II, cut: (red textured print)**
• One 2 3/4" x 42" strip. From this, cut:
    * One - 2 3/4" x 11 1/4" (2)
    * Two - 2" x 18" (5)
    * One - 2" x 11 1/4" (4)

**From Fabric III, cut: (navy & white star print)**
• One 12 1/2" x 42" strip. From this, cut:
    * Two - 12 1/2" squares for napkin.
    * One 7 1/4" square (1)

**From Fabric IV, cut: (medium blue check)**
• Two 3 1/2" wide strips for straight-grain binding.

## ASSEMBLY

Refer to diagram at right for unit numbers. Join the stripes in Section B together as shown. Join stripes in Section C together as shown.

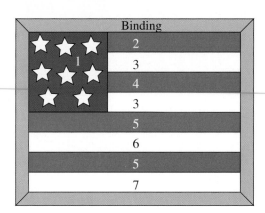

Binding
2
3
4
3
5
6
5
7

### Step 1
Stitch star fabric to top stripes, right sides together as shown.

### Step 2
Stitch star fabric and pocket fabric right sides together.

### Step 3

Pocket right side.

### Step 4
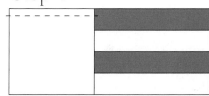
Stitch pocket facing right sides together on bottom stripes. Stitch to end and reinforce at end of stitching. Press facing upwards.

Make sure that raw edges are even. Press place mat open.

### Step 5
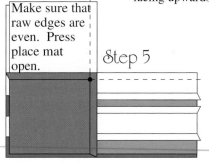

Turn over and place as shown above in an "L" with pockets and flag right sides together. Stitch as shown. Dot shows stitching into star fabric 1/4". Stitch to this point, keeping needle in down position. Pivot at this corner and stitch down side of pocket. Reinforce stitching at corner. Clip to corner.

Pin raw pocket edges together and catch into seam, as binding is applied. This closes the pocket.

## Section A

Section B

Section C

Refer to Page 8 for making and applying the wide place mat binding frame. Refer to page 11 for making our reversible napkins.

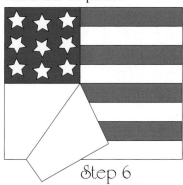

### Step 6

Our photographer, Chris was enjoying the artistry of this shot so much that he did not want us to put the sherbet in the punch bowl until he was ready. Consequently, we all forgot about the sherbet, and the punch was photographed without it! We loved the shot so much, with it's dramatic lighting and many textures, that we just had to use it.

This punch was served at our son's wedding reception, and people were standing in line for thirds and fourths. Here's the recipe:

## PINEAPPLE PASSION PUNCH

**Ingredients**

1 liter 7-Up
3 - 12 oz. cans of frozen tropical fruit concentrate
1 large can pineapple juice
1 gallon of pineapple sherbet
1 large orange, and 2 lemons for garnish

**Instructions**

Mix the liquids and concentrate together, making certain that the concentrate is thawed and mixed in well.
Add the sherbet in scoops to float on top; then garnish with sliced oranges and lemons.

# PINEAPPLE PASSION

Place mat finished size:
14" x 18". Appliqué
and pieced.

## MATERIALS FOR ONE PLACE MAT

| | | | |
|---|---|---|---|
| ▢ | Fabric I (light tan print) | Need 10" | 3/8 yard |
| ◼ | Fabric II (dark olive print) | Need 17 1/2" | 5/8 yard |
| ▨ | Fabric III (light olive print) | Need 12 1/2" | Lg. scrap |
| ◼ | Fabric IV (dk. brown textured print) | Need 1 3/4" | 1/8 yard |
| ▢ | Fabric V (medium gold pin stripe) | Need 3 1/4" | 1/4 yard |
| ▨ | Fabric VI (dark gold print) | Need 2 1/2" | 1/8 yard |
| ▨ | Fabric VII (goldish tan print) | Need 7 1/2" | 1/4 yard |
| | Backing | Need 14 1/2" x 18 1/2" | |

## CUTTING

▢ **From Fabric I, cut: (light tan print)**
• One 10" x 18" (1)

◼ **From Fabric II, cut: (dark olive print)**
• One 12 1/2" square for napkin.
• Two 3 1/2" x 42" strips for straight-grain binding.

▨ **From Fabric III, cut: (light olive print)**
• One 12 1/2" square for napkin.

◼ **From Fabric IV, cut: (dark brown textured print)**
• One 1 3/4" x 18" (2)

▢ **From Fabric V, cut: (medium gold pin stripe)**
• One 3 1/4" x 42" strip. From this, cut:
 * Two - 3 1/4" squares (3)
 * Eight - 2 1/2" x 3 1/4" (4)

▨ **From Fabric VI, cut: (dark gold print)**
• One 2 1/2" x 42" strip. From this, cut:
 * Sixteen - 2 1/2" squares (#5 prairie points)

▨ **From Fabric VII, cut: (goldish/tan print)**
• Two 7 1/2" x 9" for pineapple appliqué.

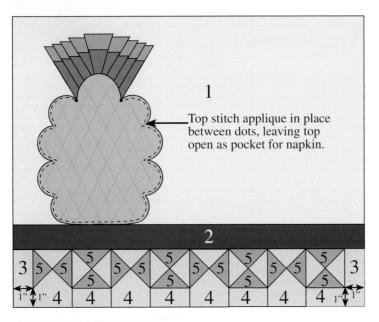

1

Top stitch applique in place between dots, leaving top open as pocket for napkin.

2

| 3 | 5 | 5 | | 5 | 5 | | 5 | 5 | | 5 | 5 | | 5 | 5 | | 5 | 5 | | 3 |
|---|---|---|---|---|---|---|---|---|---|---|---|---|---|---|---|---|---|
| | | 5 | | | 5 | | | 5 | | | 5 | | | 5 | | | 5 | |

1" 1" 4      4      4      4      4      4      4  1" 1"

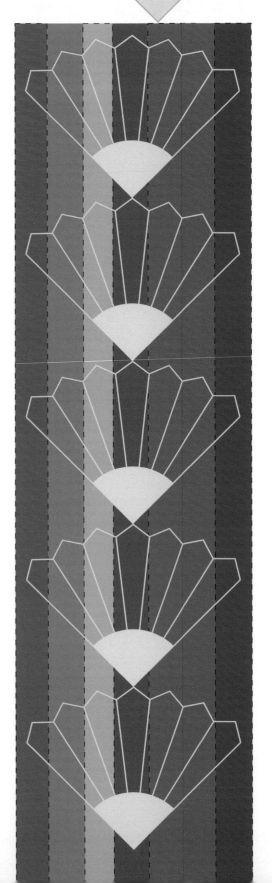

# ASSEMBLY

**Making And Applying The Prairie Points**

1. Refer to illustration below to fold the sixteen prairie points. This is a simple procedure which requires you to fold the 2 1/2" squares in half twice and lightly press.

2. Place the prairie points as shown in the place mat drawing.

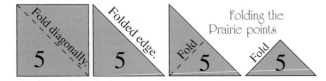

Fold diagonally. 5 | Folded edge. 5 | Folding the Prairie points — Fold 5 | Fold 5

Raw edges (the long side of the triangles) will be placed along the edge of Unit 4, with the exception of the prairie points that are vertical. The bottom point will be caught in the binding later. Pin them securely in place.

3. Join all Unit 4's together as shown, alternating the direction of the prairie points and catching them into the seam. Add Unit 3 to opposite ends of this horizontal row.

4. Join Unit 2 to top of prairie point row, again catching the prairie points into the seams. Press lightly. Join Unit 1 to top of Unit 2 as shown and press seam toward dark brown.

5. Hand tack the points of the prairie points together securely.

**Appliqué Pineapple**

1. The pineapple pattern may be found on your large pattern sheet. Follow instructions given on the pattern for sewing and turning the pineapple. Refer to place mat illustration, and place the pineapple on the top of the top of Unit 2. Pin in place, and top stitch as shown from dot to dot. Reinforce your stitching at the beginning and ending points.

**Finishing**

1. Refer to Page 8 for making and applying the wide place mat binding frame.

2. Refer to page 11 for making our reversible napkins. Fold the napkin as shown below first; then make an accordion fold. Place inside pineapple pocket.

Fold napkin as shown; then accordian fold.

# FANFARE

TABLE RUNNER.
Finishes to: 22" x 63". Pieced.
PLACE MAT
Finishes to: 14" x 18". Pieced.

## MATERIALS

| | | | |
|---|---|---|---|
| | Fabric I (gold print) | Need 11" x 18" | 3/8 yard |
| | Fabric II (light tan floral print) | Need 58 3/4" | 1 3/4 yards |
| | Fabric III (rust oriental print) | Need 12" | 3/8 yard |
| | Fabric IV (dk. rust with gold metallic) | Need 12 1/2" | 1/2 yard |
| | Fabric V (oriental print scraps) | Need 2 3/4" x 6 1/2" each scrap | |
| | 18" wide Steam-A-Seam 2 | | 1/2 yard |
| | Backing | | 1 7/8 yards |

## CUTTING

Cutting instructions shown in red indicate the quantity of units are combined and cut in two or more different places to conserve fabric.

\* *We have calculated the amount of fabric needed for the gold print appliqués. The size of the piece given is for the fan centers. Fan pattern is to be found on large pattern sheet.*

**From Fabric I, cut: (gold print)**
• One 11" x 18" for fan half and quarter circle centers.

**From Fabric II, cut: (light tan floral print)**
• Two 10 1/4" x 42" strips. From these, cut:
    * Two - 10 1/4" x 19 1/2" (3)
    * Four - 10" x 10 1/4" (2)
• Two 10" x 42" strips. From these, cut:
    * Two - 10" x 21 3/4" (1)
    * Two - 9" x 17 1/2" (double fan lining)
• One 9 1/4" x 42" strip. From this, cut:
    * Four - 9 1/4" squares (single fan lining)
• One 9" x 42" strip. From this, cut:
    * Two - 9" x 17 1/2" (add to double fan lining)

**From Fabric III, cut: (rust oriental print)**
• Six 2" x 42" strips. From these, cut:
    * Four - 2" x 30 1/2" (4) Piece 2 together to = 60 1/2"
    * Two - 2" x 22 1/2" (5)

**From Fabric IV, cut: (dk. rust with gold metallic)**
• Five 2 1/2" x 42" strips for straight-grain binding.

**From Fabric V, cut: (misc. oriental print scraps)**
• Cut eighty-four 2 3/4" x 6 1/2" for fan.

## ASSEMBLY

**1.** Using fan and fan center patterns provided on large pattern sheet, refer to our instructions for using Steam-A-Seam 2 for appliqué on page 11. Trace four half circle fan centers and four 1/4 circle fan centers on an 11" x 18" piece of Steam-A-Seam 2. Follow instructions on page 11 to fuse to Fabric I. Cut out all of the fan centers and set aside.

**2.** Cut eighty-four fan sections from oriental fabric scraps. Join the units together along the long sides. For the half circle fan, join fourteen fan units together. For the quarter circle fan, join seven fan units together. Make four of the half circle fans, and four of the quarter circle fans. Press seams to one side when fans are completed.

**3.** Beginning with the half circle fans, lay each, right sides together on 9" x 17 1/2" pieces of Fabric II. Pin together so that the fan and lining do not slip. Cut the fan lining out. While the fans are still pinned, stitch along the pointed top edge of the fan, joining the fan to its lining. Clip to dots as shown on pattern piece. Turn right side out, making certain that points are nice and sharp. Press. The fans and their linings should have raw edges even along sides and bottom. Trim, if necessary to even them up. Repeat with the quarter circle fans, using the 9 1/4" squares of Fabric II.

**4.** Pin the fans to their respective Fabric II background pieces (Units 1, 2, and 3). For the half circle fans, find the center of the background and pin the center of the fan to the center of the background piece. Long raw edges of each fan should match raw edges of background piece as shown. Refer to the diagram of the quarter square fan for correct placement on the 10" x 10 1/4" background piece.

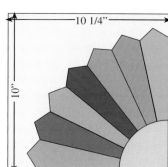

**5.** Remove the paper from the back of the fan centers. Place the fan center on top of the pinned fan, matching centers. Fan center should overlap the fan 1/4" and the long flat side of the half circle should line up with the raw edge of the background. Press the fan center in place with a hot iron on steam setting.

**6.** Place tear-away stabilizer behind the entire fan and pin in place. Satin stitch or blanket stitch the fan center around curved edge. Straight stitch "in the ditch" between each fan unit. Stitch from bottom (where fan unit meets the fan center) to the top edge of the fan unit along the seam. Reinforce your stitching at the beginning and end. Points will be loose. Raw edges of fan will be sewn into the seam when the fan sections are joined.

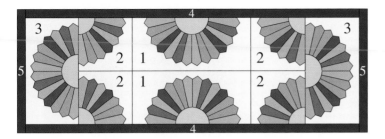

7. Join the long half circle center fan sections together as shown. Join two of the quarter circle fans as shown. Make two. Join these to opposite ends of the center fan section. Add the remaining half circle fan sections to opposite short ends of table runner.

8. Join border (4) to long sides of table runner top; then add border (5) to complete the table runner top.

9. We used flannel instead of batting for all of our tablecloths and table runners. Faye quilted lovely heart and feather designs on this table runner in a rust thread.

10. Make approximately 185" of straight-grain french fold binding, and bind the table runner.

## MATERIALS AND CUTTING FOR ONE PLACE MAT.

| Fabric I (gold print) | Need 12 1/2" | 1/2 yard |
| Fabric II (lt. tan floral print) | Need 58 3/4" | 1 3/4 yards |
| Fabric III (dk. rust/gold metallic) | Need 19 1/2" | 5/8 yard |
| Fabric IV (oriental print scraps) | Need 2 3/4" x 6 1/2" ea.scrap | |
| 18" wide Steam-A-Seam 2 | Need 3 3/4" square | scrap |
| Backing | Need 14" x 18" | |

☐ **From Fabric I, cut: (gold print)**
- One 12 1/2" square for napkin.
- One 3 3/4" square for quarter circle fan center.

☐ **From Fabric II, cut: (light tan floral print)**
- One 14" x 18" for place mat background.
- One 9 1/4" square (fan lining)

◼ **From Fabric III, cut: (dk. rust with gold metallic)**
- One 12 1/2" square for napkin.
- Two 3 1/2" x 42" strips for straight-grain binding.

▥ **From Fabric IV, cut: (misc. oriental print scraps)**
- Cut seven 2 3/4" x 6 1/2" for fan.

## ASSEMBLY

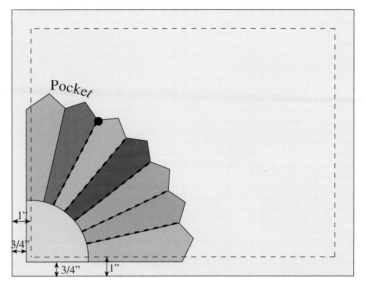

1. The fan for the place mat is assembled the same as for the table runner. Join the fan units, cut the lining and stitch it as directed in table runner, Step 4. The main difference is the placement of the fan on the 14" x 18" background, and how the pocket is made for the napkin.

2. Refer to the illustration above, and pin the fan first so that its long, flat edges are 3/4" from the edge of the place mat background. Peal the paper from the back of the fan center, and press it in place (3/4" from the edge of the background). This assures that when the place mat is bound, the fan raw edges will be sewn into the binding.

3. Place tear-away stabilizer behind the entire fan. Satin stitch or blanket stitch the fan center in place. Refer to diagram of place mat, and straight stitch "in the ditch" on the seam lines between the fan units. *Do not* stitch between the top two fan units as shown by the dot. This forms the pocket.

4. Refer to page 9 for making and applying the frame binding, and bind the place mat accordingly.

5. Instructions for making our reversible napkins are found on page 11. Sew the napkin according to the instructions. The napkin fold is shown below.

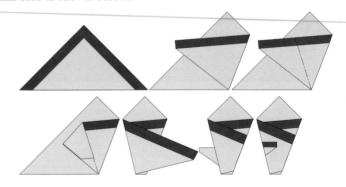

# Bird Seed Ball For Our Feathered Friends.

## Ingredients:
2 cups of bread crumbs
1/2 cup whole wheat flour
1/2 cup sugar
1 cup unsalted nuts
4-5 chopped apples
1 cup raisins or currants
1 - 8 oz. jar chunky peanut butter
1 1/2 cups bird seed
1 cup suet

## Instructions:

Mix ingredients together well. If need be, you can add more suet or some bacon drippings if dough is too crumbly. Shape into balls and freeze. Placing them into a mesh bag makes hanging easy. We use the mesh bags that oranges or onions come in.

# For The Birds

Finished size: 14" x 18" Quick pieced.
Techniques used: diagonal corners, diagonal ends, and triangle-squares.

## MATERIALS FOR ONE PLACE MAT OF EACH DESIGN

| | | | |
|---|---|---|---|
| ☐ | Fabric I (tan on ivory print) | Need 10 1/8" | 3/8 yard |
| ◩ | Fabric II (medium honey tan print) | Need 2 1/2" | 1/8 yard |
| ◼ | Fabric III (bright red print) | Need 3 7/8" | 1/4 yard |
| ◼ | Fabric IV (dark red print) | Need 2 3/4" x 8 3/4" | lg. scrap |
| ◼ | Fabric V (medium olive print) | Need 4 7/8" | 1/4 yard |
| ◻ | Fabric VI (light gold print) | Need 3" | 1/8 yard |
| ◼ | Fabric VII (dark brown print) | Need 4 1/4" | 1/4 yard |
| ◼ | Fabric VIII (medium brown print) | Need 3 7/8" | 1/4 yard |
| ◩ | Fabric IX (light tan print) | Need 2 1/8" | 1/8 yard |
| ☐ | Fabric X (white on white print) | Need 2 1/2" x 3" | Scrap |
| ◼ | Fabric XI (black on black print) | Need 12 1/2" | 1/2 yard |
| | Backing | Need 14 1/2" x 18 1/2" for each place mat | |

*\*\* If you wish to make the Chicadee only, disregard all of the "C" units, and Unit Q4 under Fabric III. If you wish to make the Cardinal only, disregard all of the "B" units, and Unit Q4 under Fabric VIII.*

All "Q" units in cutting instructions stand for place mat top. These are units that are not incorporated into the specific blocks, but are on the place mat top.

Cutting instructions shown in red indicate that the quantity of units are combined and cut in two or more different places to conserve fabric.

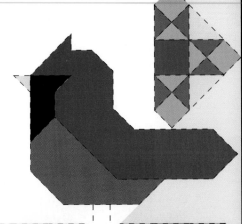

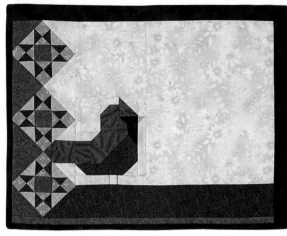

## CUTTING FOR BOTH DESIGNS

**From Fabric I, cut: (tan on ivory print)**
- One 8 7/8" x 42" strip. From this, cut:
  * Two - 8 7/8" x 11 1/8" (Q8)
  * Two - 5 1/8" x 5 3/8" (Q7)
  * One - 3 7/8" square (Q5) Cut in half diagonally.
  * One - 3" square (Q6) Cut in half diagonally.
- From scrap, cut:
  * Four - 2 7/8" squares (Q4a)
  * One - 2 1/8" x 2 3/4" (C1)
  * One - 1 3/8" x 2 7/8" (B8)
  * Two - 1 3/4" squares (B12, C4)
  * One - 1 1/2" square (C12)
  * Two - 1" x 1 3/4" (C2, C13)
- One 1 1/4" x 42" strip. From this, cut:
  * Three - 1 1/4" squares (B2b, B10a, C11a)
  * One - 1" x 1 1/4" (B13)
  * Two - 1 1/8" x 5 1/8" (B15, C15)
  * One - 1 1/8" x 2 1/4" (B1)
  * One - 1 1/8" x 1 1/2" (C7)
  * Four - 1 1/8" squares (B2a, B5a, C3a, C9a)
  * One - 1" x 5 1/8" (B16)
  * Two - 1" x 4 3/8" (B14, C14)

**From Fabric II, cut: (medium honey tan print)**
- Two 1 1/4" x 42" strips. From these, cut:
  * One - 1 1/4" x 2" (B10)
  * Forty-eight - 1 1/4" squares (A1a, A3)

**From Fabric III, cut: (bright red print)**
- One 3 7/8" x 42" strip. From this, cut:
  * One - 3 7/8" square (Q4)
  * One - 2 5/8" x 2 7/8" (C9)
  * One - 1 3/4" x 2 1/4" (C3)
  * One - 1 1/2" x 2" (C8)
  * One - 1 3/4" square (C4)
  * One - 1" x 1 1/2" (C5)

**From Fabric IV, cut: (dark red print)**
- One 2 3/8" x 8 3/4" strip. From this, cut:
  * One - 2 3/8" square (C9b)
  * One - 1 1/4" x 2 3/8" (C10)
  * One - 1 1/4" x 4 5/8" (C11)

**From Fabric V, cut: (medium olive print)**
- One 3 7/8" x 42" strip. From this, cut:
  * Two - 3 7/8" squares (Q3) Cut in half diagonally.
  * Two- 3" squares (Q2) Cut in half diagonally.
  * Six - 1 1/2" squares (A1)
- One 1" x 42" strip. From this, cut:

  * Two - 1" x 17 3/4" (Q10)

**From Fabric VI, cut: (light gold print)**
- One 2" x 42" strip. From this, cut:
  * Twenty-four - 1 1/4" x 2" (A2)
  * Two - 1" squares (B14a, C14a)

**From Fabric VII, cut: (dark brown print)**
- One 3" x 42" strip. From this, cut:
  * One 3" square (Q1) Cut in half diagonally.
  * Two - 2 5/8" x 13 1/2" (Q9)
  * Eighteen - 1 1/4" square (A2a)
- One 1 1/4" x 42" strip. From this, cut:
  * Thirty - 1 1/4" squares (add to A2a)

**From Fabric VIII, cut: (medium brown print)**
- One 3 7/8" x 42" strip. From this, cut:
  * One 3 7/8" square (Q4)
  * One - 2 5/8" x 2 3/4" (B5)
  * One - 1 3/8" x 2" (B9)

**From Fabric IX, cut: (light tan print)**
- One 2 1/8" x 42" strip. From this, cut:
  * One - 2 1/8" square (B5b)
  * One - 1 1/2" x 2 1/8" (B7)
  * One - 1 1/4" x 3 1/8" (B11)

**From Fabric X, cut: (white on white print)**
- One 1 1/2" x 2 5/8" (B3)
- Two 1" squares (B5c, B6a)

**From Fabric XI, cut: (black on black print)**
- Four 2 1/2" strips for straight-grain binding
- Two 1 1/4" x 42" strips. From this, cut:
  * Two - 1 1/4" x 17 3/4" (Q11)
  * Two - 1 1/4" x 14 1/2" (Q12)
  * One - 1 1/4" x 3 1/8" (B2)
  * Two - 1 1/4" x 1 1/2" (C6, C10a)
  * Two - 1" x 1 1/2" (B4, B6)
  * Two - 1 1/8" squares (B3a)
  * One - 1" square (C5a)

## ASSEMBLY

*Instructions given are for one block. Please note that it is of the utmost importance, with this design, to have very accurate seams. Use a consistent "scant" 1/4" seam so that blocks fit together properly.*

## Making Star Block A

1. Use diagonal corner technique to make four of Unit 2 and make one of Unit one.

2. To assemble the block, begin with the top row and join units 3-2-and 3 in a row. Make two. Join center section units by adding Unit 2 to opposite sides of Unit 1 as shown.

3. Join the rows together by adding top and bottom rows to opposite ends of center section. Make six.

Block A. Make 6
(3 for each design).
Finishes to: 3 1/2" square.

## Making Chicadee Block B

1. Use diagonal corner technique to make one each of units 2, 3, 5, 6, 10, and 14.

2. Begin assembly by joining units 3 and 4. Join Unit 2 to top of the 3-4 units; then add Unit 1 to the left side as shown.

3. Join units 6 and 7; then add Unit 5 to left side of combined 6-7 units. Join the combined 1-4 units to the top of the combined 5-7 units, matching seams carefully.

4. Join units 8 and 9. Add to left side of other combined units. Join units 10 and 11 as shown, then add these combined units to the bottom of combined units 1-9. Add diagonal corner, Unit 12 as illustrated.

5. Join units 13 and 14; then join these units to right side of Chicadee. Add Unit 16 to the top, and Unit 15 to the bottom to complete the block.

Block B. Make 1.
Finishes to: 5 1/8" x 5 3/4"

## Making Cardinal Block C.

1. Use diagonal corner technique to make one each of units 3, 5, 9, 10, 11, and 14.

2. Refer to illustration below, and use diagonal end technique to make one of Unit 10.

3. Refer to page 7 instructions for making triangle-squares, and make one triangle-square, Unit 4.

4. To assemble the block, begin by joining units 2 and 3; then add Unit 1 to left side of these combined units. Join units 5 and 6; then add triangle-square Unit 4 to top. Join these combined units to right side of combined 1-3 units as shown.

2. Join units 7 and 8. Join units 9 and 10. Stitch these combined units together in a horizontal row as illustrated. Add this row to bottom of combined units 1-6. Join Unit 11 to the bottom; then add diagonal corner, Unit 12.

3. Join units 13 and 14. Add these combined units to the right side of the Cardinal. Join Unit 15 to the bottom to complete the block.

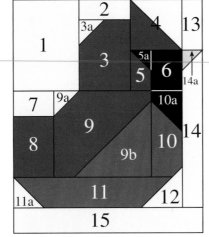

Block C. Make 1.
Finishes to: 5 1/8" x 6 1/4"

Making Unit C10

## Place Mat Assembly For Both Birds

1. Refer to the illustrations at right. To make the bird tail units, begin by using diagonal corner technique as shown in the first diagram. After diagonal corners are added to Unit Q4 and pressed, draw a diagonal line from corner to corner as shown in remaining illustrations. Cut on this line forming two triangles. Discard one.

2. For place mat top (for both birds) refer to illustrations below and join Unit Q2 to corners of two Block A's as shown. Join one to top left corner and one to bottom left corner. Join Unit Q6 to top right Block A corner, and Unit Q1 to bottom Block A right corner. Refer to diagrams, and join Unit Q5 to the bottom right corner of top Block A as shown. Join one Unit Q3 to top left corner of the bottom Block A.

3. Make a center diagonal row with remaining Block A, joining Unit Q3 to top left corner of Block A, and the Q4 tail section to the bottom right. Use accurate seams, and trim Unit Q4 if necessary. Join the three diagonal rows together, being careful to match seams.

4. Join Unit Q7 and bird block together; then add Unit Q8 to right side. Join Unit Q9 to bottom. Carefully pin the bird to the Block A row and tail section. Don't be afraid to pin, and press seams in opposite directions so that they "lock". This makes it easier to match the seams.

5. Join Unit Q10 to bottom of place mat, and Unit Q11 to the top. Add Unit Q12 to right side to complete the place mat top.

6. Cut backing and batting 1" larger than tops. Center top, right side up on batting and pin or baste the three layers together. Quilt in the ditch around patchwork. Trim backing and batting to size of top. Use 2 1/2" strips of Fabric XI to make french fold binding, and bind the place mats.

Bird tails

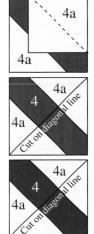

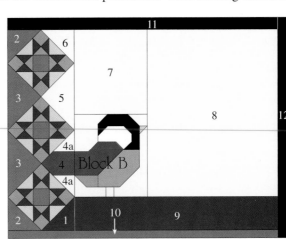

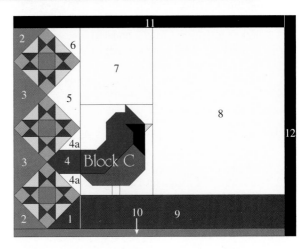

# Romance

ROMANCE TABLE RUNNER. Finishes to: 20 1/8" x 77". Pieced.

## MATERIALS

| | | | |
|---|---|---|---|
| ▧ | Fabric I (medium rose print) | Need 21" | 3/4 yard |
| ◼ | Fabric II (burgundy print) | Need 37" | 1 1/8 yards |
| ☐ | Fabric III (pink on ivory print)<br>Backing | Need 18 1/2" | 5/8 yard<br>2 1/4 yards |

## CUTTING

▧ **From Fabric I, cut: (medium rose print)**
• One 6 1/2" x 42" strip. From this, cut:
    * One - 6 1/2" x 7 1/2" (1)
    * Four - 6 1/2" squares (2)
    * Two - 2 1/2" x 4 1/2" (5)
• Four 2 1/2" x 42" strips. From these, cut:
    * Ten - 2 1/2" x 3 1/2" (3)
    * Twenty - 2 1/2" squares (4)
    * Thirty - 1 1/2" x 2 1/2" (6)
    * Six - 1 1/2" x 3 1/2" (7)
• Three 1 1/2" x 42" strips for Strip Set 1.

◼ **From Fabric II, cut: (burgundy print)**
• Seven 2 1/2" x 42" strips. Five for straight-grain binding.
  From remaining two, cut:
    * Ten - 2 1/2" squares (8)
    * Twenty-eight - 1 1/2" x 2 1/2" (9)
• Thirteen 1 1/2" x 42" strips. Seven for strip sets 1 and 2.
  From remaining six, cut:
    * Four - 1 1/2" x 29" (16) Piece two together to = 57 1/2".
    * Four - 1 1/2" x 17" (17 and 18)
    * Sixteen - 1 1/2" squares (10)

☐ **From Fabric III, cut: (pink on ivory print)**
• Five 2 1/2" x 42" strips. From these, cut:
    * Four - 2 1/2" x 4 1/2" (11)
    * Twenty - 2 1/2" x 3 1/2" (12)
    * Twenty-eight - 2 1/2" squares (13)
    * Twenty-two - 1 1/2" x 2 1/2" (14)
    * Four - 1 1/2" x 3 1/2" (15)
• Four 1 1/2" strips for Strip Set 2.

## Strawberry - Apricot Brandy Butter

### Ingredients
3 tablespoons of strawberry preserves
1 1/2 tablespoons of apricot brandy
1 stick of unsalted butter

### Instructions

In a blender (or food processor), mix the three items until smooth.  Pack butter in a decorative crock and refrigerate until ready to serve.  Garnish with strawberries on a plate.

# ASSEMBLY

**Making The Strip Sets.**

This design is much like a jig saw puzzle. It will be made in sec-

Strip Set 1. Make 3
Cut into 76
1 1/2" segments

Strip Set 2. Make 4
Cut into 104
1 1/2" segments

tions. A graphic is shown for the entire table runner which shows the section divisions so that you may see placement, and each section is illustrated separately.

**1.** Refer to our instructions on Page 6 for Strip Piecing. Drawings above show the strip sets. Assemble each strip set, and cut the segments required for each strip set.

## Section A Assembly

**1.** Section A is the section on both ends of the table runner. This illustration will be referred to later for trimming after all sections are joined. Therefore, on this section only, we show it with seam allowances on units 12, 13, 14 and 15.

**2.** The units are mirror image. Refer frequently to the graphic above when assembling the section. All strip sets will be abbreviated (s/s 1, or s/s 2). Begin by joining s/s 2 and Unit 6. Join units 10 and 14; then add Unit 15 to bottom of the 10-14 combined

Units 12, 13, and 14 show seam allowance. Cut on 45° angle on dashed line along points as shown after section is joined to both ends of table runner.

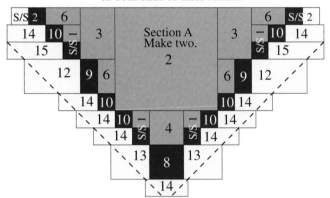

units. Join s/s 1 to side as shown, remembering that these units are mirror images. Join the s/s 2-Unit 6 combined units to the top of other combined units; then add Unit 3 to end as shown.

**3.** Join mirror image units 6, 9, and 12 in a horizontal row as shown. Join units 10 and 14 as shown. Join these combined units to the bottom of other combined units, lining Unit 10 up with Unit 6, and matching seams. Join the combined mirror image units to opposite sides of Unit 2.

**4.** For bottom of Section A, begin by once again joining units 10 and 14. Join another Unit 14 to bottom of these combined units, matching Unit 14 with Unit 10. Join s/s 1 to ends of the combined units; then add them to opposite sides of Unit 4. Join Unit 13 to opposite sides of Unit 8; then center Unit 14 at the very bottom as shown and stitch it in place. Join the 13-8-13-14 combined units to other combined units, matching Unit 4 and Unit 8 seams. Join this entire section to bottom of other combined units to complete Section A. Make two and set aside.

## Section B Assembly

**1.** To begin, join two s/s1 segments as shown. Join units 9 and 4 and add them to the combined strip set segments. Make two, referring to illustration as the second will require you to place the joined strip set segments differently. Join s/s 2 to opposite short ends of Unit 11.

**2.** Join s/s 1 to opposite sides of Unit 14 in a vertical row as

shown. Add these combined units to combined s/s 2-Unit 11, matching seams. Join s/s 1 and Unit 6 as shown. Refer to illustration for correct placement as these two are mirror images. Join these combined units to opposite ends of Unit 8; then add them to combined s/s 2-Unit 11-s/s 1-Unit 14 combination. Join the previously pieced row, made in Step 1 to top and bottom of other combined units, checking illustration for correct placement. This completes Section B. Make 4 and set aside.

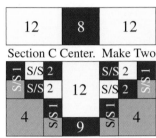

Section B. Make Four

## Section C Assembly

**1.** To make Section C Center, join Unit 12 to opposite sides of Unit 8. Make 2.

**2.** For Section C, refer to diagram and join two s/s 2 segments together; then add s/s 1 to the two combined segments. Make two that are mirror images. Join s/s 1 to Unit 4 as shown, checking drawing for correct placement of mirror image units. Add these combined units to the strip set combined units.

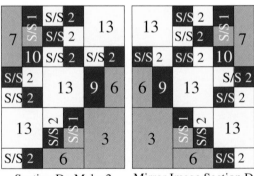

Section C Center. Make Two

Section C. Make Four.

**3.** Join Unit 9 to bottom of Unit 12; then add other combined units to opposite sides of the 9-12 combined units. Make four of Section C, and join them to opposite sides of Section C Center. This will yield two of Section C.

## Section D Assembly

**1.** Section D is a mirror image. You will make four of them, but you will want to refer to the diagrams at right frequently for correct placement of the mirror image units. Instructions are given for one of Section D.

**2.** Begin by joining the three s/s 2 segments at the top

Section D. Make 2          Mirror Image Section D Make 2

of the section in a checkerboard. Join Unit 10 to bottom of s/s 2; then add Unit 7 to side of these combined units. Join these units to s/s 2 combined units, matching seams. Join s/s 2 to bottom of Unit 13; then add these combined units to other combined units as shown.

**3.** For center of Section D, again join two s/s 2 segments. Join units 13, 9, and 6 in a row. Add the joined s/s 2 segments to the 13-9-6 combined units to complete the center. Join these combined units to the top combined units, matching seams.

**4.** For the bottom part of Section D, begin by joining s/s 1 and s/s 2 segments together as shown; then add Unit 13 to the combined segments. Join s/s 2 and Unit 6; then add them to the bottom of the strip set segments - Unit 13 combination, matching seams. Join Unit 3 to side of the other combined units to complete the bottom part. Join the bottom to the top and center combined units to complete Section D. Make four (2 are mirror images).

## Section E Assembly

**1.** To make Section E, begin by joining s/s 2 and s/s 1 segments together as shown. Refer to diagram for correct placement of mirror image units. Join these combined segments to opposite sides of Unit 4; then add Unit 2 to bottom to complete the section. Make two.

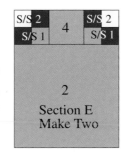

Section E
Make Two

## Section F Assembly

**1.** To assemble Section F, begin by joining two of s/s 2 as shown. Make 2. Refer to diagram for correct placement of mirror image units. Join units 9 and 13; then add them to combined strip set segments. Join Unit 12 to opposite sides of Unit 8. Join the strip set segments-Unit 13-Unit 9 combination to opposite sides of 12-8-12 units to complete Section F.

Section F. Make 2.

## Section G Assembly

**1.** Begin assembling Section G by making the center part of the section. To do so, refer to diagram at right and combine s/s 1, s/s 2, and s/s 1 segments in a row. Join Unit 10 to left side of one s/s 2 segment; then join these to top of previously combined strip set row, matching seams. Add Unit 7 to left side of the combined units, and Unit 3 to the right side.

**2.** The top and bottom portions are made the same, except for mirror image placement of the units. Instructions are for top section. Refer to the diagram for mirror image unit placement to make both top and bottom at the same time.

Section G. Make Two

**3.** Begin by joining two s/s 2 checkerboard segments together matching seams. Join units 13, 9, and 6 together; then add them to the two combined strip set segments. Join one s/s 2 segment to top of Unit 13 as shown. Join one s/s 1 segment to left side of Unit 12. Join two s/s 2 segments in a horizontal line as shown and add them to the combined s/s 2-Unit 12 combination as shown. Join the combined s/s 2-Unit 13 units to left side of s/s 2-Unit 12 combination to complete top and bottom. Join all three of the sections together to complete Section G. Make two.

## Section H Assembly

**1.** Join s/s 2 segments to opposite sides of Unit 6. Join s/s 1 segments to opposite sides of Unit 5. Join the two rows together as shown, matching seams. Make two and join them to opposite ends of Unit 1 to complete Section H. Make one Section H.

## Assembly Of The Sections.

**1.** Referring frequently to the large diagram of the table runner, begin in the center of the table runner and join Section G to opposite sides of Section H. Join Section F to top and bottom of center section.

**2.** Join Section D to opposite sides of Section E. Make two and join them to opposite ends of center section.

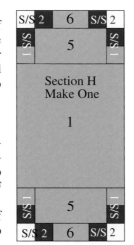

Section H
Make One

**3.** Join Section B to opposite sides of Section C as shown. Make two and add them to opposite ends of table runner. Join Section A to each end as shown.

**4.** Refer to the illustration of Section A on page 30. Trim along dashed line, beginning at corner of Unit 14 as shown. This will give you 1/4" seam allowance along pointed end.

**5.** For borders, join Unit 16 border first. Begin and end at bottom of Unit 14. Join Unit 17 border, lining it up with tip of Unit 14 as shown. Stitch in place, stitching through Unit 16 border on a 45° angle. Trim off excess. Join Unit 18 in the same manner, beginning at end of border and leaving enough tail to trim off any excess. Trim and press.

## Finishing

Faye quilted feathery designs in the large heart areas and "ditched" the patchwork. Join the five 2 1/2" strips of Fabric I, and bind with straight-grain french fold binding.

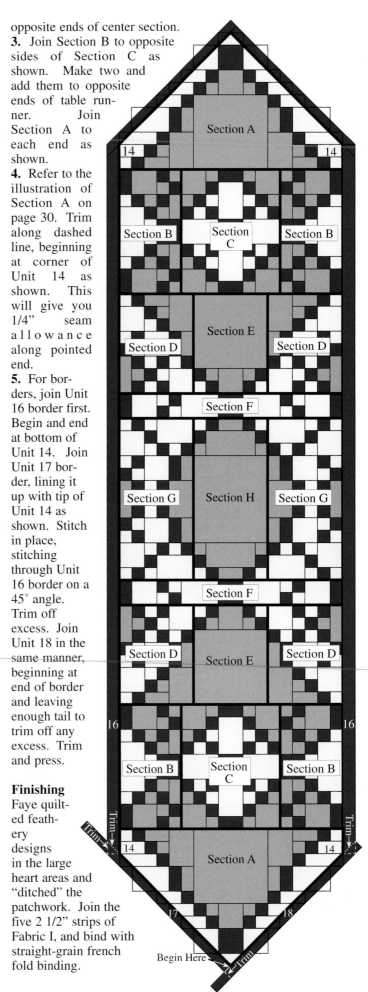

# Being The Cat's Meow Has Its Advantages!

## MATERIALS FOR ONE PLACE MAT

| | | | |
|---|---|---|---|
| | Fabric I (pink/green/ivory plaid) | Need 14" | 1/2 yard |
| | Fabric II (black on black print) | Need 19 1/2" | 5/8 yard |
| | Fabric III (white on white print) | Need 12 1/2" | 1/2 yard |
| | Fabric IV (dark green print) | Need 5" | 1/4 yard |
| | Fabric V (medium pink print) | Need 2 1/2" | 1/8 yard |
| | 1/2 yard of Steam-A-Seam 2 | | |
| | Backing | Need 14" x 18" | |

PLACE MAT. Finishes to: 14" x 18".
Pieced and appliqué.

If you haven't already met her, THIS IS ZELDA! She's the super model who has it all! Bucks, beauty and brains! See page 34 for more details!

# The Cat's Meow!

## Delecta-Bull Tuna Casserole

### Ingredients
1 - 12 oz. can of tuna
1 - 16 oz. package of noodles
1 package of frozen peas
1 small onion, chopped
1 small green pepper, chopped
20 small green olives with pimiento sliced
1 can cream of mushroom soup
1 soup can of milk
1 - 8 oz. package shredded cheddar and american cheese.

### Instructions
Cook the package of frozen peas and drain. Sauté the onions and green pepper in a small amount of cooking oil. Add the tuna, peas and sliced olives. Mix together well. Add the cream of mushroom soup and fill the empty soup can with milk, and add to the mixture.
Cook the noodles in a separate pot and drain well. Place the noodles in a casserole and pour the tuna mixture over the noodles; then mix together with a spoon.
Sprinkle the shredded cheese over the top of the tuna noodle mixture.
Cover and bake at 350 for about 20 minutes until cheese has melted and the casserole is heated through.

## CUTTING FOR ONE PLACE MAT

**From Fabric I, cut: (pink/green/ivory plaid)**
• One 14" x 18" for background

**From Fabric II, cut: (black on black print)**
• One 12 1/2" x 42" strip. From this, cut:
  * One - 12 1/2" square for napkin
  * Two -7" x 8 1/2" (to cut cat body)
  * Two - 2" x 3" (to cut ears and nose)
• Two 3 1/2" x 42" strips for straight-grain binding.

**From Fabric III, cut: (white on white print)**
• One 12 1/2" x 42" strip. From this, cut:
  * One - 12 1/2" square for napkin
  * One - 6" square (to cut head and feet)

**From Fabric IV, cut: (dark green print)**
• Two 2 1/2" x 42" strips. From these, cut:
  * Eighteen - 2 1/2" squares for prairie points

**From Fabric V, cut: (medium pink print)**
• One 2 1/2" x 42" strip. From this, cut:
  * Fifteen - 2 1/2" squares for prairie points.

# ASSEMBLY

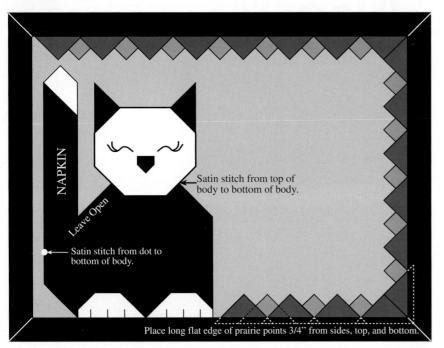

NAPKIN

Leave Open

Satin stitch from top of body to bottom of body.

Satin stitch from dot to bottom of body.

Place long flat edge of prairie points 3/4" from sides, top, and bottom.

1. The pattern for the cat appliqué will be found on the large pattern sheet. Instructions for appliqué may be found on page 11. Trace the cat's ears, nose and feet onto the Steam-A-Seam 2 as directed on page 11.

2. Follow instructions on large pattern for making the cat's body. Sew and turn as directed. Spray with spray starch. Place the cat's body on the background 1/2" in from left edge, and 3/4" up from bottom raw edge. We used small strips of Steam-A-Seam 2 along the right side of the cat's body and along the left 45° edge of his body. Press in place with a hot iron on steam setting.

3. Appliqué pieces are added in numerical order. Press ears down next. Trace eyes and whiskers on head and press down; then press the nose in place. Press the feet in place. Feet will be even with the bottom edge of the body. Raw edges at bottom will be sewn into the binding.

4. We used a medium wide satin stitch to appliqué this design. Satin stitch according to the diagram above, making sure to leave the opening in the cat's body which will be the pocket for the tail napkin. It is not necessary to appliqué the bottom of the feet.

## Making And Applying The Prairie Points

1. Refer to illustration below to fold the thirty-three prairie points. This is a simple procedure which requires you to fold the 2 1/2" squares in half twice and lightly press.

2. Place the prairie points as shown in the place mat drawing.

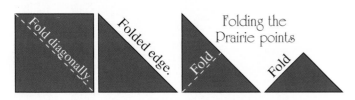

Fold diagonally.  Folded edge.  Fold.  Fold

Folding the Prairie points

Raw edges (the long side of the triangles) will be placed along the bottom, right side, and top of the place mat as shown. Begin in the bottom right corner, and work your way to the left and up the side. Place the two corner triangles and pin. Green triangles will overlap across the raw edges 1/4". Pin them in place, adjusting as you

go along. We placed the pink triangles after the green ones were secured with pins. We found this easier to center the pink triangles behind the green ones. Pin all of the prairie points in place. You may want to run a basting line along the very bottom of the prairie points to hold them when applying the binding.

3. Refer to page 8 for making the binding frame, and bind the place mat.

**The Napkin Tail**

1. Refer to page 11 for directions on how to make the reversible napkin. Illustrations below show the napkin fold.

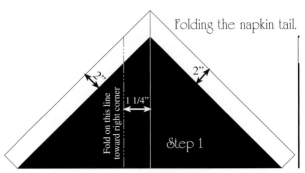

Folding the napkin tail.

2"  2"

Fold on this line toward right corner

1 1/4"

Step 1

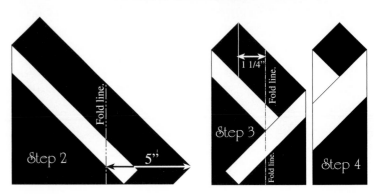

Fold line.

Step 2  5"

1 1/4"

Fold line.

Step 3

Fold line.

Step 4

Turn napkin over for tail.

Step 5

## About ZELDA!

Zelda is the fabulously rich super model who is stealing the spotlight in the greeting card, poster and calender business.

She has been named "spokes dog" for the Delta Society and is certified. Zelda will soon be on billboards throughout the world. She also has an honorary degree from Harvard - A PHD no less! "Pretty Hot Dog!" Zelda and her owner, Carol Gardner help people laugh at themselves and realize that things "could be worse." Zelda is a "heavy breathing, short legged, pudgy chick who has dozens of people waiting for her paw print!"

Her Mother's Day card features Zelda in a flowered house dress and Poodle wig with caption: "One Tough Mother!"

Zelda has appeared on many of the major talk shows, including Good Morning America. She earns more a year than President Bush, Brad Pitt and Julia Roberts put together!

Be sure to get inspirational laughs to cheer your day. Visit Zelda's Web site at: www.zeldawisdom.com

# Northwoods

## Holiday Pumpkin Torte Squares

### Ingredients

**CRUST**
1 1/2 cups graham cracker crumbs
1/3 cup sugar
1/2 cup butter or margarine

**CREAM CHEESE FILLING**
2 eggs
3/4 cup sugar
1 package (8 oz.) softened cream cheese.

**PUMPKIN LAYER**
1 - 16 oz. can pumpkin
3 egg yolks
1/2 cup milk
1/2 cup sugar
1/2 teaspoon salt
1 teaspoon ground cinnamon
1 envelope unflavored gelatin
1/4 cup cold water
1 - 8 oz. carton Cool Whip
Additional whipped topping

### Instructions

Combine crust ingredients and press into the bottom of a 13" x 9" x 2" baking pan. Combine eggs, sugar and cream cheese in a mixing bowl, beating until smooth. Spread over the crust. Bake at 350 for 20-25 minutes or until top appears set. Set aside and cool. Combine pumpkin, egg yolks, milk, sugar, salt and cinnamon in a saucepan. Cook on medium, stirring constantly, until mixture thickens. Remove from heat. Dissolve gelatin in water and add to saucepan. Fold in Cool Whip. Spread over cooled cream cheese filling. Chill for at least 4 hours. Cut into squares and serve with a dollop of whipped topping.

Torte keeps well for several days in the refrigerator. Serves 12-15.

"Party Of Four" square tablecloth finishes to: 57 1/2" square. "Button Them Down" extensions finish to: 18" x 57 1/2". Complete tablecloth ("Party Of Ten") finishes to: 57 1/2" x 93".
Quick Pieced.

# MATERIALS FOR SQUARE TABLECLOTH

| | | | |
|---|---|---|---|
| ☐ | Fabric I (light tan print) | 74 3/4" | 2 1/4 yards |
| ◼ | Fabric II (rust print) | 32 5/8" | 1 yard |
| ◼ | Fabric III (dark gold print) | 24" | 3/4 yard |
| ◻ | Fabric IV (light gold print) | 11 1/8" | 1/4 yard |
| ☐ | Fabric V (ivory print) | 10" | 3/8 yard |
| ◼ | Fabric VI (dark brown print) | 5 7/8" | 1/4 yard |
| ◼ | Fabric VII (dark brown check) | 5 3/8" | 1/4 yard |
| ◼ | Fabric VIII (dark olive print) | 8" | 3/8 yard |
| ◼ | Fabric IX (medium olive print) | 11 3/4" | 3/8 yard |
| ◻ | Fabric X (light olive print) | 13" | 1/2 yard |
| ◼ | Fabric XI (dark forest green) Backing | 8" | 3/8 yard 3 3/4 yards |

## CUTTING

All "Q" units in cutting instructions stand for tablecloth top. These are units that are not incorporated into the specific blocks, but are on the place mat top.

Cutting instructions shown in red indicate that the quantity of units are combined and cut in two or more different places to conserve fabric.

**From Fabric I, cut: (light tan print)**
• One 7" x 42 1/2" strip. From this, cut:
   * Two - 7" squares (Q1) Cut in half diagonally
   * Two - 3 1/2" x 12 1/2" (Q13) stack this cut
   * Sixteen - 2" x 3 1/2" (A5) stack this cut
• One 5 7/8" x 42" strip. From this, cut:
   * Sixteen - 2 1/8" x 5 7/8" (A1)
• One 4 3/8" x 42" strip. From this, cut:
   * Four - 4 3/8" squares (Q2) Cut in half diagonally
   * Sixteen - 2" x 2 3/4" (A4) stack this cut
• Four 3 3/4" x 42" strips. From these, cut:
   * Four - 3 3/4" x 21 3/4" (Q9)
   * Four - 3 3/4" x 18 1/2" (Q7)
• One 3 5/8" x 42" strip. From this, cut:
   * Two - 3 5/8" squares (Q3) Cut in half diagonally
   * Four - 1 5/8" x 12 1/2" (Q4) stack this cut
   * Eight - 1" x 2 1/4" (D4) stack this cut
• Three 3 1/2" x 42" strips. From these, cut:
   * Eighteen - 3 1/2" x 6 1/2" (A7, Q12)
• Four 2 1/4" x 42" strips for Strip Set 1
• One 2 1/8" x 42" strip. From this, cut:
   * Sixteen - 2 1/8" squares (D1a)
• Three 2" x 42" strips. From these, cut:
   * Sixteen - 2" x 4 1/4" (A6)
   * Sixteen - 2" squares (A3b)
   * Sixteen - 1 3/8" x 2" (A3a)
• One 1 1/2" x 42" strip. From this, cut:
   * Sixteen - 1 1/2" squares (D1b)
• Three 1 1/4" x 42" strips. From these, cut:

   * Sixteen - 1 1/4" x 5 3/8"(D2)
• Six 1" x 42" strips for Strip Set 1.

**From Fabric II, cut: (rust print)**
• One 2 5/8" x 42" strip. From this, cut:
   * Five - 2 5/8" squares (B3)
   * Ten - 2 3/8" squares (B2) Cut in half diagonally
• Six 3" x 42" strips for straight-grain binding.
• Six 2" x 42" strips. From these, cut:
   * Four - 2" x 20" (Q6)
   * Two - 2" x 19" (Q10)
   * Four - 2" x 18 1/2" (Q5)
   * Two - 2" x 12 1/2" (Q11)
   * Four - 2" x 3 3/4" (Q8)

**From Fabric III, cut: (dark gold print)**
• Three 4 1/4" x 42" strips. From these, cut:
   * Twenty-one - 4 1/4" squares (B4, C4) Cut in an X
   * Fourteen - 2 5/8" squares (B1, C5)
• Two 2 5/8" x 42" strips. From these, cut:
   * Twenty-two - 2 5/8" squares (add to B1, C5)
   * Thirteen - 2" squares (C2)
• Three 2" x 42" strips. From these, cut:
   * Fifty-one - 2" squares (add to C2)

**From Fabric IV, cut: (light gold print)**
• Two 4 1/4" X 42" strips. From these, cut:
   * Sixteen - 4 1/4" squares (C3) Cut in an X
   * Five - 2 5/8" squares (B1)
• One 2 5/8" x 42" strip. From this, cut:
   * Fifteen - 2 5/8" squares (B1)

**From Fabric V, cut: (ivory print)**
• Two 2 5/8" x 42" strips. From these, cut:
   * Twenty - 2 5/8" squares (B1)
• Two 2 3/8" x 42" strips. From these, cut:

---

# MOCHA MINT LATTE

*Ingredients*

*1 3/4 oz. Chocolate Syrup*
*1/2 oz. Cream de Menthe Syrup*
*2 oz freshly brewed hot espresso*
*Hot steamed/foamed milk*
*Whipped cream*
*Chocolate topping powder*
*Shaved chocolate*

*Pour chocolate syrup into a 12 oz. cup and add the espresso. Fill with hot steamed/foamed milk. Stir once, lifting from the bottom to bring the syrups up.*
*Top with whipped cream and sprinkle with chocolate topping powder and shaved chocolate.*

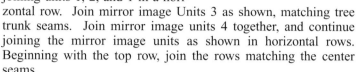

* Thirty-two - 2 3/8" squares (C1) Cut in half diagonally.

**From Fabric VI, cut: (dark brown print)**
- One 5 7/8" x 42" strip. From this, cut:
  * Eight - 1" x 5 7/8" (D3)
  * Eight - 1 3/4" x 2 1/8" (A2)
  * Sixteen - 1 1/8" x 2" (A3a)

**From Fabric VII, cut: (dark brown check)**
- One 5 3/8" x 42" strip. From this, cut:
  * Eight - 3 3/4" x 5 3/8" (D1)

**From Fabric VIII, cut: (dark olive print)**
- Four 2" x 42" strips. From these, cut:
  * Sixteen - 2" x 6 1/2" (A3)
  * Sixteen - 2" squares (A4b)

**From Fabric IX, cut: (medium olive print)**
- One 5 3/4" x 42" strip. From this, cut:
  * Sixteen - 2" x 5 3/4" (A4a)
  * Five - 2" x 4 1/4" (A6a)
- Three 2" x 42" strips. From these, cut:
  * Eleven - 2" x 4 1/4" (add to A6a)
  * Thirty-two - 2" squares (A5b, A7b)

**From Fabric X, cut: (light olive print)**
- Two 3 1/2" x 42" strips. From these, cut:
  * Sixteen - 3 1/2" squares (A7a)
  * Five - 2" x 5" (A5a)
- Three 2" x 42" strips. From these, cut:
  * Eleven - 2" x 5" (add to A5a)
  * Sixteen - 2" squares (A6b)

**From Fabric XI, cut: (dark forest green)**
- Eight 1" x 42" strips for Strip Set 1.

## ASSEMBLY

**Assembling Tree Block A**

1. Use diagonal corner technique to make two mirror image units 3 and 7. Refer to diagram below for making Unit 3. First join the A3a units from Fabrics I and VI together forming a 2" square. This square is now used as a diagonal corner, forming the top part of the tree trunk. Place this square as shown in diagram, right sides together on Unit 3 and stitch the diagonal.

2. Use diagonal end technique to make two mirror image units 4, 5, and 6. Refer to diagram at top right, and

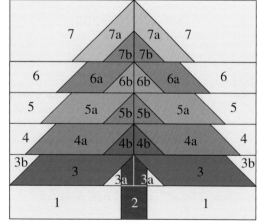

Block A. Make 8 (4 for corners)
Make 4 for extensions.
Tree finishes to 11 1/8" x 12 1/2"
Corner Tree Block finishes to:
12 1/2" square.

Making mirror image Unit A3

make all of the units in this manner. Diagonal corners are added after diagonal ends have been joined and pressed.

3. To assemble the trees, begin by joining units 1, 2, and 1 in a horizontal row. Join mirror image Units 3 as shown, matching tree trunk seams. Join mirror image units 4 together, and continue joining the mirror image units as shown in horizontal rows. Beginning with the top row, join the rows matching the center seams.

4. The illustrations below show how to make the corner trees. Follow the diagrams and instructions.

**Assembling Star Blocks B and C**

1. Refer to the star block diagrams on page 39, and the instructions in the gold box beneath them. Follow the directions and diagrams for making Unit 1 for Block B.

2. Both star blocks are assembled diagonally. To assemble Block B, begin by

## Making the corner tree

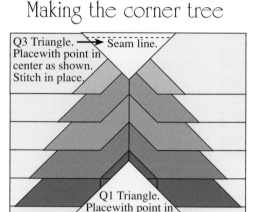

Corner Block A. Make 4

joining Unit 2 triangles to each dark gold corner of Unit 1. Add triangle Unit 4 to opposite sides of Unit 1 as shown. Make two of these rows. For center row, join combined units 1 and 2 to opposite sides of center square, Unit 3. Join the three diagonal rows together to complete the star. Make 5 stars.

3. To assemble Block C star, again assembly will be on the diagonal. Join all triangle Units 1 to Unit 2 as shown. Join the long edge of triangle Unit 3 to the 1-2 combined units. For the side diagonal rows, add triangle Unit 5 to opposite sides of combined units 1-2-3. Make two.

4. For the star center, join combined units 1-2-3 to opposite sides of Unit 4 center square. Join the three rows together, referring to Block C diagram for correct placement. Make sixteen of Block C.

**Making The Pine Needle Strip Set**

1. Refer to the illustrations of Strip Set 1 on page 39. For strip piecing instructions, refer to page 6. Join 1" strips of Fabrics I and

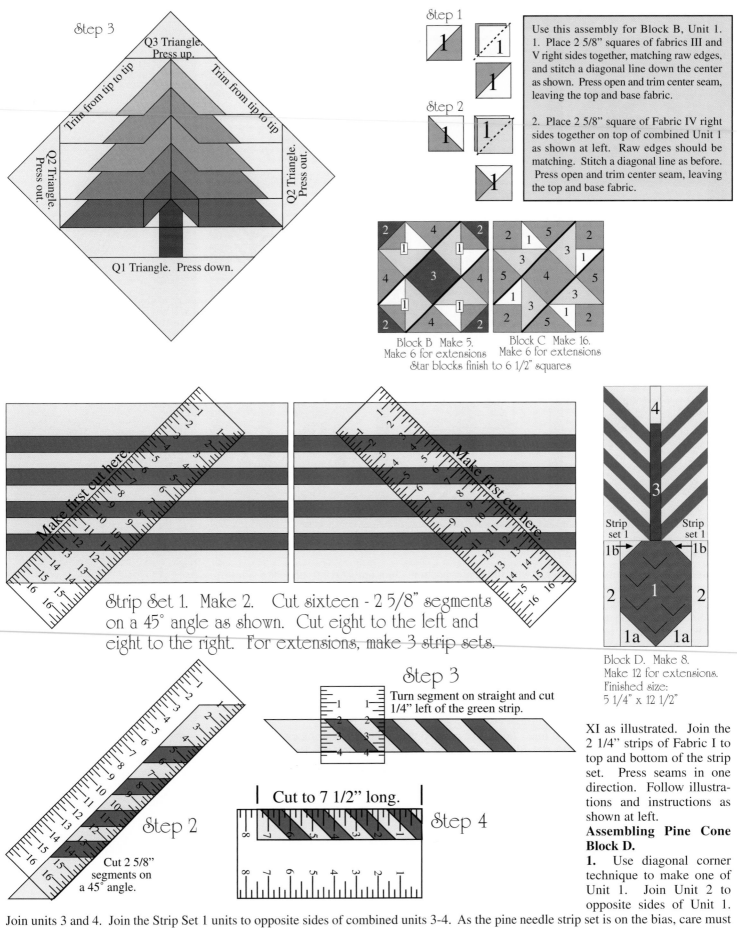

**Step 3**

Q3 Triangle. Press up.

Trim from tip to tip

Trim from tip to tip

Q2 Triangle. Press out.

Q2 Triangle. Press out.

Q1 Triangle. Press down.

**Step 1**

**Step 2**

Use this assembly for Block B, Unit 1.
1. Place 2 5/8" squares of fabrics III and V right sides together, matching raw edges, and stitch a diagonal line down the center as shown. Press open and trim center seam, leaving the top and base fabric.

2. Place 2 5/8" square of Fabric IV right sides together on top of combined Unit 1 as shown at left. Raw edges should be matching. Stitch a diagonal line as before. Press open and trim center seam, leaving the top and base fabric.

Block B  Make 5.
Make 6 for extensions

Block C  Make 16.
Make 6 for extensions
Star blocks finish to 6 1/2" squares

Make first cut here

Make first cut here

Strip Set 1.  Make 2.  Cut sixteen - 2 5/8" segments on a 45° angle as shown.  Cut eight to the left and eight to the right.  For extensions, make 3 strip sets.

Block D.  Make 8.
Make 12 for extensions.
Finished size:
5 1/4" x 12 1/2"

**Step 2**

Cut 2 5/8" segments on a 45° angle.

**Step 3**

Turn segment on straight and cut 1/4" left of the green strip.

Cut to 7 1/2" long.

**Step 4**

XI as illustrated. Join the 2 1/4" strips of Fabric I to top and bottom of the strip set. Press seams in one direction. Follow illustrations and instructions as shown at left.

**Assembling Pine Cone Block D.**

**1.** Use diagonal corner technique to make one of Unit 1. Join Unit 2 to opposite sides of Unit 1.

Join units 3 and 4. Join the Strip Set 1 units to opposite sides of combined units 3-4. As the pine needle strip set is on the bias, care must be taken to press the strip set gently and avoid handling too much. Pinning will be very helpful when joining the strip set to the other units. Press seams towards center. Make 8 pine cone blocks.

# TABLECLOTH ASSEMBLY

**1.** To assemble the tablecloth, begin with the center section. Join units Q12 to opposite sides of one star Block B; then add Unit Q13 to top and bottom as shown. Join a pine cone Block D to opposite ends of center section; then add tree Block A to opposite ends. Join Unit Q4, pine cone Block D, and Unit 11 together. Make two and join them to opposite ends of center section.

**2.** For side sections, refer to illustration for correct placement of all units and blocks. Begin by joining two of star Block C together. Make eight of these joined star blocks. Join the "on point" tree to one side of the star blocks. Refer to diagram for correct placement of tree block. Make four. Join Block B to one side of the remaining joined star Blocks C; then add them to the bottom of the combined tree and star Blocks C, matching corner seams. Referring again to diagram above, join Unit Q5 to one side of the combined "on point" trees and stars; then join Unit Q6 as shown to complete the tablecloth corners.

**3.** Join Units Q7 and Q8. Make four. Join these units to the corner tree/star blocks as shown. Join pine cone Block D, Unit Q4, tree Block A, and another pine cone Block D. Refer to the illustration for correct placement of the pine cone blocks as they face opposite directions. Join Unit Q9 to opposite sides of the pine cone/tree section; then add Unit Q10 to the bottom as shown.

**4.** Join the "on point" tree corner sections to opposite sides of the pine cone/tree section to complete the sides. Join the side sections to opposite sides of the center to complete the tablecloth top.

**5.** Our quilter, Julie quilted swirl designs in the large open spaces and "ditched" all of the patchwork. She also added some cute squirrel's and birds.

**6.** After your tablecloth has been quilted, trim the backing and flannel filling, leaving 1 1/4" all the way around the tablecloth. The binding is 3" wide. Refer to page 8 and apply binding as directed. The 1 1/4" will provide the "filling" for the binding.

**7.** Measure in 1" from each end of the binding on opposite sides of the tablecloth and mark. As there will be take-up with the quilting, measuring the entire length of the tablecloth will be important. Mark for buttonholes about 3" x 3 1/2" apart, and stitch buttonholes in the center of the binding to accommodate a flat 3/4" wooden button.

# "Button Down" Extensions

Each extension finishes to: 18" x 57 1/2". With both extensions added, tablecloth
finishes to approximately 57 1/2" x 93". Quick Pieced.

# MATERIALS FOR TWO EXTENSIONS

| | | | |
|---|---|---|---|
| ⬜ | Fabric I (light tan print) | Need 59 3/4" | 1 3/4 yards |
| ⬛ | Fabric II (rust print) | Need 30 1/8" | 1 yard |
| ⬛ | Fabric III (dark gold print) | Need 17 3/4" | 3/4 yard |
| ⬛ | Fabric IV (light gold print) | Need 6 7/8" | 1/4 yard |
| ⬜ | Fabric V (ivory print) | Need 7 5/8" | 1/4 yard |
| ⬛ | Fabric VI (dark brown print) | Need 5 7/8" | 1/4 yard |
| ⬛ | Fabric VII (dark brown check) | Need 7 1/2" | 1/4 yard |
| ⬛ | Fabric VIII (dark olive print) | Need 4" | 1/4 yard |
| ⬛ | Fabric IX (medium olive print) | Need 6" | 1/4 yard |
| ⬛ | Fabric X (light olive print) | Need 5 1/2" | 1/4 yard |
| ⬛ | Fabric XI (dark forest green) | Need 12" | 1/2 yard |
| | Backing | | 1 7/8 yards |

Approximately 32 - 3/4" flat wooden buttons.

### ⬛ From Fabric II, cut: (rust print)
- One 2 5/8" x 42" strip. From this, cut:
  * Six - 2 5/8" squares (B3)
- Eight 3" x 42" strips for straight-grain binding.
- One 2 3/8" x 42" strip. From this, cut:
  * Twelve - 2 3/8" squares (B2) Cut in half diagonally.

### ⬛ From Fabric III, cut: (dark gold print)
- Two 4 1/4" x 42" strips. From these, cut:
  * Twelve - 4 1/4" squares (B4, C4) Cut in an X
  * Twelve - 2 5/8" squares (B1, C5)
- Two 2 5/8" x 42" strips. From these, cut:
  * Eighteen - 2 5/8" squares (add to B1, C5)
- Two 2" x 42" strip. From this, cut:
  * Twenty-four - 2" squares (C2)

### ⬛ From Fabric IV, cut: (light gold print)
- One 4 1/4" x 42" strip. From this, cut:
  * Six - 4 1/4" squares (C3) Cut in an X
  * Six - 2 5/8" squares (B1)
- Two 2 5/8" x 42" strips. From these, cut:
  * Eighteen - 2 5/8" squares (add to B1)

### ⬜ From Fabric V, cut: (ivory print)
- Two 2 5/8" x 42" strips. From these, cut:
  * Twenty-four - 2 5/8" squares (B1)
- One 2 3/8" x 42" strip. From this, cut:
  * Twelve - 2 3/8" squares (C1) Cut in half diagonally.

### ⬛ From Fabric VI, cut: (dark brown print)
- One 5 7/8" x 42" strip. From this, cut:
  * Twelve - 1" x 5 7/8" (D3)
  * Four - 1 3/4" x 2 1/8" (A2) stack this cut
  * Eight - 1 1/8" x 2" (A3a) stack this cut

### ⬛ From Fabric VII, cut: (dark brown check)
- Two 3 3/4" x 42" strips. From these, cut:
  * Twelve - 3 3/4" x 5 3/8" (D1)

# CUTTING

### ⬜ From Fabric I, cut: (light tan print)
- One 12 1/2" x 42" strip. From this, cut:
  * Four - 3 5/8" x 12 1/2" (Q8)
  * Twelve - 1 3/4" x 12 1/2" (Q9)
- Two 6 1/2" x 42 1/2" strips. From these, cut:
  * Two - 6 1/2" squares (Q10)
  * Eight - 3 1/2" x 6 1/2" (A7)
  * Four - 2 1/4" x 6 1/2" (Q11)
  * Eight - 2 1/8" x 5 7/8" (A1)
  * Nineteen - 1 1/4" x 5 3/8" (D2)
- One 4 1/4" x 42" strip. From this, cut:
  * Eight - 2" x 4 1/4" (A6)
  * Eight - 2" x 3 1/2" (A5)
  * Eight - 2" squares (A3b) stack this cut
- Six 2 1/4" x 42" strips for Strip Set 1.
- Two 2 1/8" x 42" strips. From these, cut:
  * Twenty-four - 2 1/8" squares (D1a)
  * Twenty - 1 1/2" squares (D1b)
- One 2" x 42" strip. From this, cut:
  * Eight - 2" x 2 3/4" (A4)
  * Eight - 1 3/8" x 2" (A3a)
  * Four - 1 1/2" squares (add to D1b)
- One 1 1/4" x 42" strip. From this, cut:
  * Five - 1 1/4" x 5 3/8" (add to D2)
  * Twelve - 1" x 2 1/4" (D4)
- Nine 1" x 42" strips for Strip Set 1.

---

### ⬛ From Fabric VIII, cut: (dark olive print)
- Two 2" x 42" strips. From these, cut:
  * Eight - 2" x 6 1/2" (A3)
  * Eight - 2" squares (A4b)

### ⬛ From Fabric IX, cut: (medium olive print)
- Three 2" x 42" strips. From these, cut:
  * Eight - 2" x 5 3/4" (A4a)
  * Eight - 2" x 4 1/4" (A6a)
  * Sixteen - 2" squares (A5b, A7b)

### ⬛ From Fabric X, cut: (light olive print)
- One 3 1/2" x 42" strip. From this, cut:
  * Eight - 3 1/2" squares (A7a)
  * Seven - 2" squares (A6b)
- One 2" x 42" strip. From this, cut:
  * Eight - 2" x 5" (A5a)
  * One - 2" square (add to A6b)

### ⬛ From Fabric XI, cut: (dark forest print)
- Twelve 1" x 42" strips for Strip Set 1.

# ASSEMBLY

**1.** Refer to instructions on pages 38-40 for making blocks A, B, C, and D. Make four Block A trees, six star Block B, six star Block C, and twelve of pine cone Block D.

**2.** Refer to instructions on pages 38 and 39 for making Strip Set 1. Make three of Strip Set 1, and cut pine needle segments as shown for tablecloth.

**3.** To assemble the extensions, begin at the top and join Unit Q9 to one Block D; then add star Block B to side as shown. Make two.

**4.** Join Unit 8 to tree Block A. Join Unit 9 to side of pine cone Block D as shown; then add Unit Q11 to end of the combined Q9-Block D combination. Join these to the Q8-Block A combined units. Make two of these for each end of the extension.

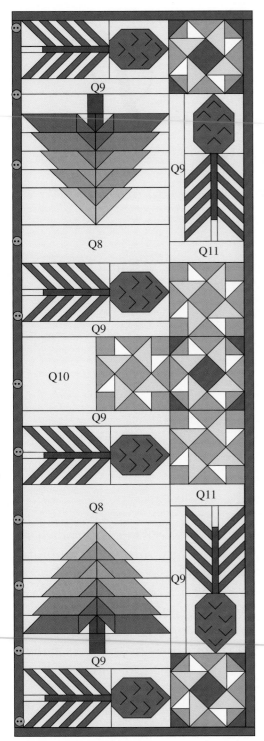

**Extension. Make two.**

Instructions for 2 chair backs and seats. Chair backs finish to: 16 3/4" x 22 1/2". Seat cushion finishes to: 16" square.

## MATERIALS FOR CHAIR BACKS & SEATS

| | | | |
|---|---|---|---|
| ☐ | Fabric I (light tan print) | Need 25 3/8" | 7/8 yard |
| ■ | Fabric II (rust print) | Need 35 3/4" | 1 1/8 yards |
| ▨ | Fabric III (dark gold print) | Need 15 1/2" | 1/2 yard |
| ☐ | Fabric IV (light gold print) | Need 8 1/2" | 3/8 yard |

**5.** For center of extension, begin by joining Unit Q10, Block C, and Block B in a horizontal row. Refer to diagram at left and join Unit Q9 to side of pine cone Block D; then add star Block C to the end. Make two that are mirror images as shown. Join these three rows together, matching the star seams; then add the end tree sections to complete the extension top. Make two of the extensions, and quilt with the same designs used on the square tablecloth.

**6.** See instructions for binding on page 40, steps 6 and 7. Bind extensions in same manner. Sew the flat wooden buttons to match the buttonholes on the tablecloth. When a large group comes for dinner, just "Button Down!"

| | | | |
|---|---|---|---|
| ☐ | Fabric V (ivory print) | Need 6 3/4" | 1/4 yard |
| ■ | Fabric VI (dark brown print) | Need 2 1/2" x 6 1/2" Lg. scrap | |
| ▨ | Fabric VII (dark brown check) | Need 6" x 8": Lg. scrap | |
| ▨ | Fabric VIII (medium olive print) | Need 2 5/8" 1/8 yard | |
| ■ | Fabric IX (dark forest green print) | Need 4" Backing | 1/4 yard 1 1/4 yards |

**\*\*If you have made the tablecloth, you should have enough strip set segments left for the chair backs. If so, please ignore the strip set cutting instructions.**

## CUTTING

☐ **From Fabric I, cut: (light tan print)**
- One 7 5/8" X 42" strip. From this, cut:
  * Four - 7 5/8" squares (Q9) Cut in half diagonally
  * Four - 1 1/4" x 5 3/8" (D2)
  * Four - 2 1/8" squares (D1a)
  * Four - 1 1/2" squares (D1b)
- One 5 1/4" x 42" strip. From this, cut:
  * Two - 5 1/4" squares (Q2)
  * Two - 3 1/2" x 5 1/4" (Q3)
  * Two - 5" x 11" (Q1)
  * Two - 1" x 2 1/4" (D4)
- One 5" x 42" strip. From this, cut:
  * Two - 5" x 11" (add to Q1)
- Two 2 1/4" x 42" strips for Strip Set 1.
- Three 1" x 42" strips for Strip Set 1.

■ **From Fabric II, cut: (rust print)**
- One 5 1/4 x 42" strip. From this, cut:
  * Four - 2" x 5 1/4" (Q5)
  * Four - 5 1/8" squares (Q6) Cut in half diagonally
- Seven 2 1/2" x 42" strips for straight-grain binding.
- One 2" x 42" strip. From this, cut:
  * Four - 2" x 11" (Q4)
- Six 1 1/2" x 42" strips for chair back and seat ties.

▨ **From Fabric III, cut: (dark gold print)**
- Two 4 1/4" x 42 1/4" strips. From these, cut:
  * Ten - 4 1/4" squares (C4) Cut in an X
  * Forty - 2" squares (C2) stack this cut
- Four 1 3/4" x 42" strips. From these, cut:
  * Four - 1 3/4" x 16 1/2" (Q11)
  * Four - 1 3/4" x 14" (Q10)

☐ **From Fabric IV, cut: (light gold print)**
- Two 4 1/4" x 42" strips. From these, cut:
  * Ten - 4 1/4" squares (C3) Cut in an X

☐ **From Fabric V, cut: (ivory print)**
- Two 2 3/8" x 42" strips. From these, cut:
  * Twenty - 2 3/8" squares (C1) Cut in half diagonally
- Two 1" x 42" strips. From these, cut:
  * Four - 1" x 10" (Q8)
  * Four - 1" x 9" (Q7)

■ **From Fabric VI, cut:** (dark brown print)
• Two - 1" x 5 7/8" (D3)

■ **From Fabric VII, cut:** (dark brown check)
• Two - 3 3/4" x 5 3/8"

■ **From Fabric VIII, cut:** (medium olive print)
• One 2 5/8" x 42" strip. From this, cut:
  * Ten - 2 5/8" squares (C4)

■ **From Fabric IX, cut:** (dark forest green print)
• Four 1" x 42" strips for Strip Set 1.

## ASSEMBLY

**1.** Refer to illustration below of the star block. This block is made the same as Block C. The only difference is the color of fabric used in the center of the star. All units for this star in the cutting instructions are Block C units.

**2.** Refer to pages 38 and 39 for making the star and pine cone blocks. Make ten star blocks for the chair back and seat, and two pine cone blocks.

**3.** To assemble the chair back, begin by joining units Q2 and Q5. Join units Q3 and Q5. Refer to the diagram for proper placement of the units, and join the Q2-Q5 and Q3-Q5 combined units to the top and bottom of the pine cone block.

Make 10 for chair cover

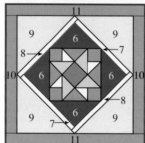

**4.** For the side sections of the chair back, join units Q1 and Q4; then add the star block to top and bottom of the combined units, checking illustration for correct placement of the Q1-Q4 mirror images. Join the side sections to the center section to complete the chair back.

**Seat Assembly**
**1.** Join triangle Unit Q6 to sides of star block as shown. Join Q7 border to opposite sides; then add Q8 border to remaining sides. Join triangles Q9 around the center star section. Join border Q10 to opposite sides as shown; then add Q11 borders to complete the seat.

**Finishing**
**1.** We used a double layer of batting for the back and seat to give a nice puffy effect. Stitch all patchwork "in the ditch." Julie quilted tall pine trees in the long side panels of the chair back and bunnies in the open spaces on the seat.
**2.** Make continuous straight-grain binding from 2 1/2" strips of Fabric II, and bind the back and the seat. To make the ties, cut 18" long lengths from the 1 1/2" strips of Fabric II. With right sides together, stitch the ties, leaving an opening to turn. Turn right side out and close the opening with a small piece of Steam-A-Seam 2. Top stitch along each edge and across the bottom of each strip. Stitch the ties on the back side of the back and seat by finding the center, and stitching down the center to hold them firmly in place.

# Pinky Floyd

Lorie's Quick & Easy Carrot Cake

### Ingredients

1 - 2 layer white cake mix, any brand dry
1 cup Miracle Whip
4 eggs
2/3 cup cold water
1 teaspoon cinnamon
1 teaspoon ground cloves
1 teaspoon nutmeg
1/2 teaspoon ginger
2 teaspoon allspice
2 1/2 cups shredded, grated carrots
1/4 cup chopped walnuts (optional)
1/2 cup raisins

### Instructions

Combine mix, Miracle Whip, eggs, water, and spices. Stir in carrots, raisins and walnuts.
Bake 35 minutes at 350.
Makes a 10" and a 6" round or 9" x 13" cake.
For variety, you may also add 1/4 cup coconut and 1/4 cup crushed pineapple.
Frost with cream cheese frosting. If making a 2-layer cake, fill with cream cheese frosting.

# MATERIALS

| | | | |
|---|---|---|---|
| □ | Fabric I  (white print) | Need 14" x 18" | 1/2 yard |
| ■ | Fabric II  (pink marble print) | Need 12 1/2" | 1/2 yard |
| ■ | Fabric III  (bright orange print) | Need 10" | 3/8 yard |
| ■ | Fabric IV  (dark green print) | Need 3" x 31/2" | scrap |
| □ | Fabric V  (light pink floral print) | Need 12 1/2" | 1/2 yard |
| ■ | Fabric VI  (salmon textured print) | Need 5 1/2" x 9 1/2" | scrap |
| | 18" wide Steam-A-Seam 2 | | 1/2 yard |
| | Backing | Need 14" x 18" | |

CUTTING AND ASSEMBLY INSTRUCTIONS
ON FOLLOWING PAGE.

MATERIALS & CUTTING FOR ONE PLACE
MAT.  Finishes to:  14" x 18".  Appliqué.

45

*We have calculated the amount of fabric needed for the appliqués, and the pieces to be cut from the fabric size given are indicated with each cut. Appliqué pattern pieces are found on large pattern sheet.*

## CUTTING

**From Fabric I, cut: (white print)**
• One 14" x 18" for background.

**From Fabric II, cut: (pink marble print)**
• One 12 1/2" square for napkin.
• Two 5" x 5 3/4" for #10 head
• One 6 3/4" x 7" for #5 body

**From Fabric III, cut: (bright orange print)**
• One 3" x 8" for #8 carrot.
• Two 3 1/2" x 42" strips for straight-grain binding.

**From Fabric IV, cut: (dark green print)**
• One 3" x 3 1/2" for #7 carrot top.

**From Fabric V, cut: (light pink floral)**
• One 12 1/2" square for napkin.
• One 4" x 5" for #6 stomach.

**From Fabric VI, cut: (salmon textured print)**
• One 5 1/2" x 9 1/2" for #1 and 2 arms, #3 and 4 feet, and #9 hand.

## ASSEMBLY

**1.** Refer to page 8 for making and applying our straight-grain binding frame. Cut your backing and batting and bind as instructed. This is done first, as parts of the bunny appliqué extend into the binding frame.

**2.** The pattern for the bunny appliqué will be found on the large pattern sheet. Instructions for appliqué may be found on page 11. Trace all of the bunny body parts onto the Steam-A-Seam 2 as directed on page 11, cutting the sizes of fabrics and Steam-A-Seam 2 to the sizes given in the cutting instructions above.

**3.** Follow instructions on large pattern for making Pinky's head. Sew and turn as directed. Spray with spray starch. Place the appliqué units on the background in numerical order. Some pieces will overlap other pieces. When putting the head in place, we used small strips of Steam-A-Seam 2 along the edges of the head that are not to be left open. When the entire bunny is placed in the correct position, press in place using a hot iron on steam setting.

**4.** Refer to the photograph for placement of Pinky. One foot and one arm will extend into the binding frame.

**5.** We used a medium wide satin stitch to appliqué this design. Satin stitch according to the photo. We used a blanket stitch around the bunny's cheeks. Use a straight stitch and top stitch Pinky's head in place along edges. Leave the opening between dots. Reinforce your stitching at all dots. This becomes the slide through pocket for the napkin ears.

**6.** Refer to page 11 for making the reversible napkin. Fold napkin as shown below and bring through opening in Pinky's head. A little pinch pleat or tuck makes the ears even cuter near the head.

Folding the reversible napkin ears.

# Tom

*Turkey Tetrazzini*

*Ingredients*
2 tablespoons cornstarch
1 1/4 cups skim milk
3/4 cup turkey broth or chicken bouillon
1/2 teaspoon salt
1/2 teaspoon garlic powder
1/8 teaspoon pepper
1/4 cup grated parmesan cheese
2 tablespoons white wine
1 - 4 oz can mushrooms, drained
1 - 2 oz jar chopped pimiento, drained
4 oz pasta cooked and drained
2 cups cooked turkey cut into 1/2" cubes
2 tablespoons sliced almonds

*Instructions*
In 3-quart saucepan over medium heat, combine cornstarch, milk, broth, salt, garlic powder and pepper. Bring mixture to a boil, stirring constantly. Remove from heat and stir in cheese, wine, mushrooms, pimiento, pasta and turkey.
Pour turkey mixture into lightly greased 9" square casserole. Top with almonds. bake at 375 - 25 minutes or until mixture bubbles and top is browned.

# MATERIALS

| | Fabric I (red feather print) | Need 13" x 16 1/2" | 1/2 yard |
|---|---|---|---|
| | Fabric II (brown tweed) | Need 4" x 8 1/2" | 1/4 yard |
| | Fabric III (dark brown check) | Need 13" | 1/2 yard |
| | Fabric IV (light gold dot) | Need 3" x 6" | scrap |
| | Fabric V (bright gold textured print) | Need 3" x 7 1/4" | scrap |
| | Fabric VI (bright gold print) | Need 1 1/4" x 2" | scrap |
| | Fabric VII (bright red print) | Need 1 3/4" x 3" | scrap |
| | Fabric VIII (metallic feathered print) | Need 12 1/2" | 1/2 yard |
| | Fabric IX (pale gold print) | Need 14" x 18" | 1/2 yard |

Scraps of solid black, medium blue, and white for eyes.
18" wide Steam-A-Seam 2 — 1/2 yard
Backing — Need 14" x 18"

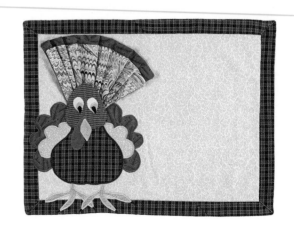

CUTTING AND ASSEMBLY INSTRUCTIONS
ON FOLLOWING PAGE.

47

\* *We have calculated the amount of fabric needed for the appliqués, and the pieces to be cut from the fabric size given are indicated with each cut. Appliqué pattern pieces are found on large pattern sheet.*

## CUTTING

**From Fabric I, cut: (red feather print)**
- One 12 1/2" square for napkin
- Two 4" x 5 1/2" for side feathers #2

**From Fabric II, cut: (brown tweed)**
- Two 4" x 4 1/4" for head #5

**From Fabric III, cut: (dark brown check)**
- One 5" x 6" for turkey body.

**From Fabric IV, cut: (light gold dot)**
- Two 3" squares for #3.

**From Fabric V, cut: (bright gold textured print)**
- One 3" x 7 1/2" for #1.

**From Fabric VI, cut: (bright gold print)**
- One 1 1/4" x 2" for #7

**From Fabric VII, cut: (bright red print)**
- One 1 3/4" x 3" for #6.

**From Fabric VIII, cut: (metallic feathered print)**
- One 12 1/2" square for napkin.

**From Fabric IX, cut: (pale gold print)**
- One 14" x 18" for place mat background.

## ASSEMBLY

**1.** Refer to page 8 for making and applying our straight-grain binding frame. Cut your backing and batting and bind as instructed. This is done first, as parts of the turkey appliqué extend into the binding frame.

**2.** The pattern for the turkey appliqué will be found on the large pattern sheet. Instructions for appliqué may be found on page 11. Trace all of the turkey body parts onto the Steam-A-Seam 2 as directed on page 11, cutting the sizes of fabrics and Steam-A-Seam 2 to the sizes given in the cutting instructions above.

**3.** Follow instructions on large pattern for making Tom's head. Sew and turn as directed. Opening may be closed with a small piece of Steam-A-Seam 2. Spray with spray starch. Place the appliqué units on the background in numerical order. Some pieces will overlap other pieces. When putting the head in place, we used small strips of Steam-A-Seam 2 along the edges of the head that are not to be left open. When the entire turkey is placed in the correct position, press in place using a hot iron on steam setting.

**4.** Refer to the photograph for placement of Tom. His feet, and one feather will extend into the binding frame.

**5.** We used a medium wide satin stitch to appliqué this design. Satin stitch according to the photo. Use a straight stitch and top stitch Tom's head in place along edges from dot to dot as shown on large pattern. Reinforce your stitching at all dots. This becomes the pocket for the napkin tail.

**6.** Refer to page 11 for making the reversible napkin. Fold napkin as shown on page 11, and then accordion fold the napkin for the tail feathers.

# Tea Party Treats

## Crispy Sugar Angels

### Ingredients
1/2 cup butter or margarine, softened
1/2 cup shortening
1/2 cup sugar
1/2 cup packed brown sugar
1 egg
1 teaspoon vanilla extract
2 cups all purpose flour
1 teaspoon baking soda
1 teaspoon cream of tartar
1/2 teaspoon salt
water
brown sugar

### Instructions
In a mixing bowl, cream the butter, shortening, sugars, egg and vanilla until light and fluffy. Sift dry ingredients together. Add to creamed mixture, mixing until blended. Shape into large marble size balls. Dip half of the ball into the water; then into the brown sugar. Place the sugared side up on ungreased cookie sheets. Bake at 400 for 6 minutes or until done. Makes 4 dozen.

## Strawberry Cream Cookies

### Ingredients

1 cup butter, softened
1 cup sugar
1 package (3 ounces) cream cheese, softened
1 tablespoon vanilla extract
1 egg yolk at room temperature
2 1/2 cups all purpose flour
Strawberry jam at room temperature

### Instructions
In a mixing bowl, cream butter, sugar and cream cheese. Add vanilla and egg yolk. Mix well. Add flour and blend. Chill. Shape dough into 1" balls and place on an ungreased cookie sheet. Using a floured thimble, press a hole in the center of the cookie and fill with 1/4 teaspoon jam. Bake at 350 for 10-12 minutes. Makes about 5 dozen.

# Tea Party

You Are Invited To

A Bridal Shower
Celebration For:

Miss Kendall Kookogey

Sunday, June 10, 2002,
1:30 p.m.
At:

The Apple Orchard Inn
Durango, Colorado

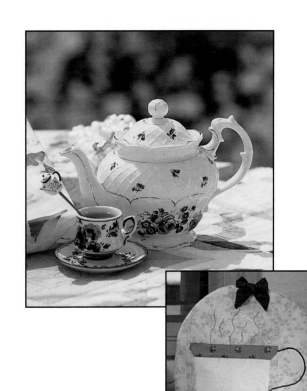

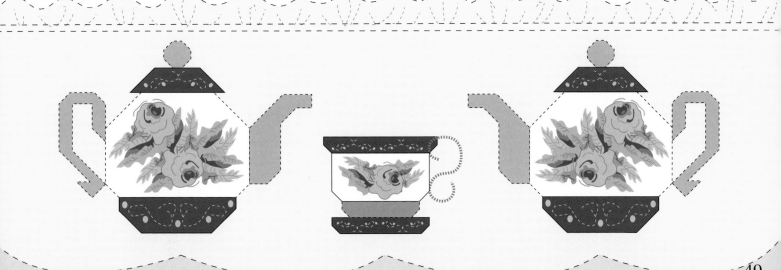

# MATERIALS

| | | | |
|---|---|---|---|
| ☐ | Fabric I  (white on white print) | 79 3/8" | 2 3/8 yards |
| ☐ | Fabric II  (white on ivory print) | 7 1/8" | 1/4 yard |
| ☐ | Fabric III  (light blue print) | 11 5/8" | 3/8 yard |
| ☐ | Fabric IV  (medium blue print) | 11 7/8" | 1/2 yard |
| ☐ | Fabric V  (navy print) | 11 1/8" | 3/8 yard |
| ☐ | Fabric VI  (medium yellow print) | 59" | 1 3/4 yards |
| ☐ | Fabric VII  (light green print) | 29" | 1 yard |
| ☐ | Fabric VIII  (medium green print) | 6" | 1/4 yard |
| ▥ | Fabric IX  (assorted medium blue and navy print scraps) Backing | | 4 1/4 yards |

# CUTTING

All "Q" units in cutting instructions stand for tablecloth top. These are units that are not incorporated into the specific blocks, but are on the tablecloth top.

Cutting instructions shown in red indicate that the quantity of units are combined and cut in two or more different places to conserve fabric.

**From Fabric I, cut: (white on white print)**
- Three 5 1/8" x 42" strips. From these, cut:
  * Thirty-two - 3 1/2" x 5 1/8" (A16)
  * Twenty-four - 1 1/8" x 2 1/8" (A20) stack this cut.
- Two 5" x 42" strips. From these, cut:
  * Thirty-two - 2" x 5" (A23)
  * Thirty-nine - 1 1/2" squares (A6a, A8a, A14a) stack this cut.
- One 4 3/8" x 42" strip. From this, cut:
  * Eight - 4 3/8" squares (Q2, Q7) Cut in half diagonally to equal sixteen triangles
  * Eight -1 1/8" x 2 1/8" (add to A20)
- Four 4" x 42" strips. From these, cut:
  * Thirty-two - 2 1/2" x 4" (A15)
  * Thirty-two - 1 1/2" x 4" (A7)
  * Twenty-four - 2" x 3" (A10) stack this cut.
- Two 3 5/8" x 42" strips. From these, cut:
  * Thirty-two - 1 7/8" x 3 5/8" (A22)
  * Thirty - 1 1/2"squares (add to 1 1/2" sq. above)
- One 3" x 42" strip. From this, cut:
  * Eight - 2" x 3" (add to A10)
  * Thirty-four - 1 1/2" squares (add to 1 1/2" sq. above)
- One 2 5/8" x 42" strip. From this, cut:
  * Thirty-two - 1" x 2 5/8" (A18)
- Two 2 1/2" x 42" strips. From these, cut:
  * Thirty-two - 1 7/8" x 2 1/2" (A4)
- Six 1 1/2" x 42" strips. From these, cut:
  * Sixty-four - 1 1/2" x 2 1/2" (A17, A21) stack this cut
  * Fifty-seven - 1 1/2" squares (add to 1 1/2" sq. above)
- Six 1 1/8" x 42" strips. Two for Strip Set 1. From remaining strips, cut:
  * Sixty-four - 1 1/8" squares (A3a)
  * Sixty-four - 1 1/8" x 1 1/4" (A2)

**From Fabric II, cut: (white on ivory print)**
- Two 1 7/8" x 42" strips. From these, cut:
  * Thirty-two - 1 7/8" x 2 1/2" (A3)
- Three 1 1/8" x 42" wide strips. From these, cut:
  * Thirty-two - 1 1/8" x 1 1/4" (A12)
  * Sixty-four - 1 1/8" squares (A11b, A14b)

**From Fabric III, cut: (light blue print)**
- Five 1 7/8" x 42" strips. From these and scrap, cut:
  * Thirty-two - 1 7/8" x 4" (A6)
  * Sixty-four - 1 1/4" x 1 7/8" (A5)
- Two 1 1/8" x 42" wide strips. From these, cut:
  * Sixty-four - 1 1/8" squares (A4a)

**From Fabric IV, cut: (medium blue print)**
- Five 1 7/8" x 42" wide strips. From these, cut:
  * Sixty-four - 1 7/8" x 2 1/2" (A11, A14)
  * Thirty-two - 1 1/4" x 1 7/8" (A13)
- Two 1 1/4" x 42" strips. From these, cut:
  * Sixty-four - 1 1/4" squares (A5a)

**From Fabric V, cut: (navy print)**

- Two 2" x 42" strips. From these, cut:
  * Thirty-two - 2" x 2 1/8" (A19)
  * Thirty- 1" squares (18a)
- Four 1 1/2" x 42" strips. From these, cut:
  * Thirty-two - 1 1/2" x 2 5/8" (A17a)
  * Thirty-two - 1 1/2" x 1 5/8" (A21a)
- One 1 1/8" x 42" strip. From this, cut:
  * Thirty-two - 1 1/8" squares (A20a)
  * Two - 1" squares (add to 18a)

**From Fabric VI, cut: (medium yellow print)**
- One 8 1/8" x 42" strip. From this, cut:
  * Four - 8 1/8" squares (Q5) Cut in half diagonally.
  * Eight - 1 1/4" x 4" (B10) stack this cut.
  * Thirty-two - 1" squares (B1a, C1a, C2a, C4a, C5a) stack this cut.
- One 5 1/2" x 42" strip. From this, cut:
  * Eight - 1" x 5 1/2" (C6)
  * Four - 5 1/4" x 7 1/2" (C7)
- Two 3 3/8" x 42" strips. From these, cut:
  * Eight - 3 3/8" x 5 3/8" (B4)
  * Eight - 3 3/8" x 4 1/2" (B5)
  * Twelve - 1" squares (add to 1" sq. above) stack this cut.
- Two 2 1/2" x 42" strips. From these, cut:
  * Eight - 2 1/2" x 4 3/4" (B19)
  * Eight - 2 1/2" x 3 7/8" (B21)
  * Eight - 1 3/4" x 2 3/8" (B14)
- Four 2 3/8" x 42" strip. From these, cut:
  * Forty - 2 3/8" squares (B6a, B7a, B16a)
  * Sixteen - 2" x 2 3/8" (B2)
  * Seven - 2 1/8" x 4 7/8" (B9)
- One 2 1/8" x 42" strip. From this, cut:
  * One - 2 1/8" x 4 7/8" (add to B9)
  * Nineteen - 1 7/8" squares (B3a, B20a)
- One 1 7/8" x 42" strip. From this, cut:
  * Thirteen - 1 7/8" squares (add to 1 7/8" sq. above)
  * Eight - 1 5/8" x 1 7/8" (B13)
- Eight 1 1/2" x 42" strips. From these, cut:
  * Eight - 1 1/2" x 35" (Q8) Join two together.
- Three 1 3/8" x 42" strip. From this, cut:
  * Eight - 1 3/8" squares (B7b)
  * Four - 1 3/8" x 13" (Q3)
  * Eight - 1 1/4" x 1 5/8" (B18)
  * Sixteen - 1 1/8" squares (B11a, B15a)
- Two 1 1/4" x 42" strip for Strip Set 1. From second strip, cut:
  * Thirty-two - 1 1/4" squares (A1, B6b, B17a)
- One 1 1/8" x 42" strip. From this, cut:
  * Eight - 1 1/8" x 1 1/2" (C3)
  * Twenty - 1" squares (add to 1" sq. above)

**From Fabric VII, cut: (light green print)**
- One 11 1/4" x 42" strip. From this, cut:
  * One - 11 1/4" square (Q1) Cut diagonally into X.
  * Four - 1 1/4" x 29 1/4" (Q4) stack this cut
  * Five - 1 1/4" x 27" (Q6) Piece 2 together to = 53 1/2"
- Eleven 1 1/2" x 42" strips. From these and scrap, cut:
  * Eight- 1 1/2" x 36" (Q9) Join 2 together to = 71 1/2".
  * Thirty-two - 1 1/2" x 4" (A8)
  * Thirty-two - 1 1/2" squares (A23a)
- One 1 1/4" x 42" strip. From this, cut:
  * Three - 1 1/4" x 27" (add to Q6) Piece two together to = 53 1/2".

**From Fabric VIII, cut: (medium green print)**
- Four 1 1/2" x 42" strips. From these, cut:

51

* Thirty-two - 1 1/2" x 2" (A9)
* Sixty-four - 1 1/2" squares (A11a, A16a)

**From Fabric IX, cut:** (scraps from assorted blue, navy and white with blue prints)

* Please note that these are for teapot and tea cups. Cutting is for one block only.
- One 2" square (B1)  teapot top
- One 2 3/8" x 3 1/8" (B16)  handle
- One 1 7/8" x 5 3/4" (B3)  teapot lid
- One 1 1/4" x 2" (B17)  handle
- One 6 3/8" x 8 1/2" (B6)  teapot center
- One 1 1/2" x 7 1/2" (C1)  tea cup top
- One 2 1/2" x 7" (B20)  teapot bottom
- One 3 1/2" x 6 1/2" (C2)  tea cup center
- One 2 3/8" x 5 5/8" (B7)  teapot spout
- One 1 1/2" x 5 1/4" (C4)  tea cup bottom
- One 1 1/4" x 2 1/8" (B8)  spout
- One 1 1/2" x 6 1/2" (C5)  saucer
- Two 1 1/4" square (B9a, B14a)  spout
- One 1 1/4" x 2 1/2" (B11)  teapot handle
- One 1 1/8" x 1 5/8" (B12)  handle
- One 1 1/4" x 3 3/4" (B15)  handle

## ASSEMBLY

### Flower Block A Assembly

**1.** Refer to page 6 instructions for strip piecing. Join strips as shown from fabrics I and VI. Press all seams in the same direction. Cut into segments as directed.

**2.** To begin Block A, use diagonal corner technique to make two each of units 3, 4, 5, 6, 8, 11, 14, 16, 18, 20, and 23. Refer frequently to diagram for correct placement of mirror image units 5, 11, 14, 16, and 23.

**3.** Use diagonal end technique to make two each of units 17 and 21. See diagrams at right for correct placement of diagonal end units.

**4.** To assemble Block A, begin in the center of the block and join Unit 3 to opposite sides of the strip set units 1 and 2. Join mirror image Units 5 to opposite sides of Unit 4 as shown; then join Unit 6 to combined units 4-5 as shown.

**5.** Join units 7 and 8. Join units 9 and 10. Join units 12 and 13. Add mirror image Unit 11 to top of combined units 12-13 and mirror image Unit 14 to the bottom. Join combined units 9-10 to sides of combined units 11-12-13, referring to diagram frequently for correct placement of mirror image units. Carefully match the Unit 9 and 11 seams. Join combined units 7-8 to top of combined units 9-14; then

|  |
|------|
| 1 1/8" |
| 1 1/4" |
| 1 1/8" |

Strip Set 1 for units 1 and 2. Make 1. Cut into 16 - 1 1/4" segments

Making Unit A17

Making Unit A21

add Unit 15 to bottom. Join this combination of units to opposite sides of flower center.

**5.** To make the bluebell, join units 19 and 20. Refer to illustration of Block A. These units are not mirror images, but will simply be turned when completed. Join Unit 18 to combined 19-20 units as shown; then add Unit 21. Join Unit 17 to complete the bluebell. Join Unit 22 to bottom of bluebell; then add mirror image Unit 23 to bluebell side as shown. Join mirror image Unit 16 to top to complete the bluebell section. Join this section to opposite sides of flower to complete Block A. **Note: We used a triple stitch for the small bluebell stem which is to be stitched in a coordinating green thread.

### Making Teapot Block B.

**1.** Refer to large diagram of tablecloth top. The teapots are mirror images. Make four facing left, and four facing right.

**2.** Use diagonal corner technique to make one of units 1, 3, 6, 7, 9, 11, 14, 15, 16, 17, and 20.

**3.** To assemble the teapot, join units 2, 1, and 2 in a horizontal row; then add Unit 3 to the bottom of the row. Join Unit 4 to left side of combined units, and Unit 5 to right side as shown. Join units 8 and 9; then add Unit 7 to right side of these combined units. Add Unit 10 to the bottom; then join Unit 6 to right side of the spout combined units.

**4.** For the handle, begin by joining units 12 and 13; then add Unit 11 to left side. Join Unit 14 to bottom; then add Unit 15 to right side of the combined units. Join Unit 16 to bottom of combined handle units. Join units 17 and 18 as shown; then add them to the bottom of the handle, matching seams.

Add the handle section to the teapot and spout section. Join the teapot top section to the center section.

**5.** For teapot bottom, join units 19, 20, and 21 in a row. Add this row to teapot bottom to complete the block. Make 8 different combinations.

### Making Tea Cup Block C

**1.** Use diagonal corner technique to make one of units 1, 2, 4, and 5.

**2.** To assemble the tea cup, join

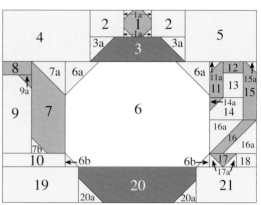
Block B. Make 4. Finishes to: 11 1/4" x 14 5/8"

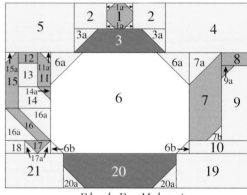
Block B. Make 4

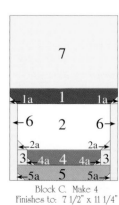
Block C. Make 4
Finishes to: 7 1/2" x 11 1/4"

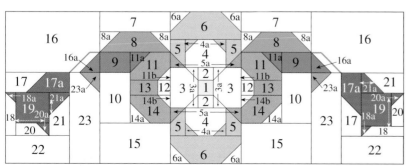
Block A. Make 16. Finishes to: 8" x 20 1/4"

units 3 and 4 as shown; then add Unit 2 to the top of the combined units, and Unit 5 to the bottom. Join Unit 6 to opposite sides; then add Unit 1 to top of the tea cup. Join Unit 7 as shown to complete the tea cup. The handle will be drawn and stitched after the teapot row is assembled.

## Tablecloth Assembly

**1.** Refer to the diagram of the tablecloth on page 54. The table-cloth is put together in triangular sections. There are twelve of flower Block A that will require you to trim off either the right or left side, depending upon their placement in the triangle. The cen-

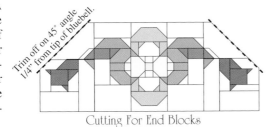

Trim off on 45° angle 1/4" from tip of bluebell.

Cutting For End Blocks

ter flowers will require you to cut both ends as shown in the illustration below. The ends will be trimmed on a 45° angle. Place your ruler 1/4" from the bluebell tip as shown. Line it up so that you establish the 45° angle and trim.

**2.** To assemble the tablecloth, these directions will tell you how to assemble one of the triangular sections, as all four are the same. For center, join Unit Q3 to Unit Q1 to bottom long edge of Q1 triangle and trim ends on a 45° angle. Trim the flower on both sides as shown at left. Add triangle Unit Q2 to each straight side below blue-bell. Join Q4 strip and once again trim ends on 45° angle.

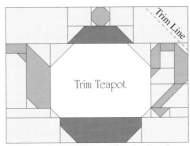

Trim Line

Trim Teapot

Trim as shown. 1/4" from 45° angle of handle.

53

**3.** For the teapots, use the 45° angle of the handle, and place your ruler so that it is lined up 1/4" out from the handle and trim as shown on all teapots. Add triangle Q5 to handle side of teapot on flat edge as shown in tablecloth top drawing. Make a row of two teapots and one tea cup as shown. Draw the handle on the tea cup and use a triple stitch and navy thread to stitch the handle. Placing stabilizer behind the stitching helps to keep it from buckling or distorting.

**4.** Join the teapot/tea cup row to the bottom of Q4 border strip. Join Q6 border strip and trim ends on a 45° angle. Refer to large diagram and join three flowers in a row. End flowers will be trimmed as shown in illustration on page 53, with one end only being trimmed on each flower. Join Q7 triangle to short bluebell flat side. Add the flower row to the tablecloth bottom. Join Q5 border; then add Q6 border and trim both even with flower row on 45° angle. Make 4 sections and join them together, matching seams.

TEA PARTY CHAIR BACKS AND SEATS. Back finishes to: 16 1/2" x 20". Seat finishes to: 15" x 15 1/4"

## MATERIALS

| | | |
|---|---|---|
| ☐ | Fabric I  (white on white print) | Need 22 3/8" |
| | 3/4  yard | |
| ☐ | Fabric II  (white on ivory print) | Need 2 1/2" |
| | 1/8 yard | |
| ☐ | Fabric III  (light blue print) | Need 68" |
| | 2 yards | |
| ☐ | Fabric IV  (medium blue print) | Need 5" |
| | 1/4 yard | |
| ☐ | Fabric V  (navy print) | Need 36 3/4" |
| | 1 1/8 yards | |
| ☐ | Fabric VI  (medium yellow print) | Need 4 1/4"" |
| | 1/4 yard | |
| ☐ | Fabric VII  (light green print) | Need 3" |
| | 1/8 yard | |

☐ Fabric VIII  (medium green print)  Need 3"
1/8 yard

## CUTTING

☐ **From Fabric I, cut:  (white on white print)**
- One 5" x 42" strip. From this, cut:
  * Twelve - 1 1/2" x 5" (A17)
  * Twelve - 1 1/2" x 4" (A7)
  * Twelve - 1 1/2" squares (A6a, A8a, A14a)
- One 3 1/2" x 42" strip. From this, cut:
  * Twelve - 1 1/2" x 3 1/2" (A16)
  * Twelve - 2" x 3" (A10)
- Two 3 1/8" x 42" strips. From these, cut:
  * Four - 3 1/8" x 13" (Q6)
  * Two - 1 1/2" x 13" (Q1)  stack this cut
  * Twenty-four - 1 1/2" squares (add to A6a, A8a, A14a)
- Two 2 1/2" x 42" strips. From these, cut:
  * Twelve - 2 1/2" x 4" (A15)
- One 1 7/8" x 42" strip. From this, cut:
  * Twelve - 1 7/8" x 2 1/2" (A4)
- One 1 1/2" x 42" strip. From this, cut:
  * Twenty-four - 1 1/2" squares (add to A6a, A8a, A14a)
- One 1 1/8" x 42" strip. From this, cut:
  * Twenty-four - 1 1/8" squares (A3a)
  * Twelve - 1 1/8" x 1 1/4" (A2)

☐ **From Fabric II, cut:  (white on ivory print)**
- One 2 1/2" x 42" strip. From this, cut:
  * Twelve - 1 7/8" x 2 1/2" (A3)
  * Twelve - 1 1/8" x 1 1/4" (A12) stack this cut
- One 1 1/8" x 42" strip. From this, cut:
  * Twenty-four - 1 1/8" squares (A11b, A14b)

☐ **From Fabric III, cut:  (light blue print)**
- Eight 8 1/2" x 42" strips. From these, cut:
  * Eight- 8 1/2" x 25 1/2" (bow)  Piece two together.
  * Twelve - 1 7/8" x 4" (A6)
  * Twenty-four - 1 1/4" x 1 7/8" (A5)
      * Twenty-four - 1 1/8" squares (A4a)

☐ **From Fabric IV, cut:  (medium blue print)**
- Two 1 7/8" x 42" strips. From these, cut:
  * Twenty-four - 1 7/8" x 2 1/2" (A11, A14)
  * Twelve - 1 1/4" x 1 7/8" (A13)
- One 1 1/4" x 42" strip. From this, cut:
  * Twenty-four - 1 1/4" squares (A5a)

☐ **From Fabric V, cut:  (navy print)**
- Seven 2 1/2" x 42" strips for straight-grain binding.
- Four 2" x 42" strips. From these, cut:
  * Four - 2" x 20 1/2" (Q5)
  * Four - 2" x 14" (Q4)
  * Two - 1 3/4" x 13 1/4" (Q7)
- Three 1 3/4" x 42" strips. From these, cut:
  * Four - 1 3/4" x 15 1/2" (Q8)
  * Two - 1 3/4" x 13 1/4" (add to Q7)
- Four 1 1/2" x 42" strips. From these, cut:
  * Four - 1 1/2" x 32" for chair seat ties.

☐ **From Fabric VI, cut:  (medium yellow print)**
- One 1 1/4" x 42" strip. From this, cut:
  * Six - 1 1/4" squares (A1)

* Two - 1" x 13" (Q2)
- Three 1" x 42" strips. From these, cut:
  * Four - 1" x 17 1/2" (Q3)
  * Two - 1" x 13" (add to Q2)

 **From Fabric VII, cut:** (light green print)
- Two 1 1/2" x 42" strips. From these, cut:
  * Twelve - 1 1/2" x 4" (A8)
  * Twelve - 1 1/2" squares (A17a)

 **From Fabric VIII, cut:** (medium green print)
- Two 1 1/2" x 42" strips. From these, cut:
  * Twelve - 1 1/2" x 2" (A9)
  * Twenty-four - 1 1/2" squares (A11a, A16a)

# ASSEMBLY

## Flower Block A Assembly

1. Refer to page 52 for strip set instructions. You will have plenty of the strip set left for the chair backs and seats. Cut six 1 1/4" segments for units 1 and 2.

2. This flower Block A is the same as the flower block for the quilt, with the exception of the bluebells. Please use these piecing instructions, as some of the units are different. To begin Block A, use diagonal corner technique to make two each of units 3, 4, 5, 6, 8, 11, 14, 16, and 17. Refer frequently to diagram for

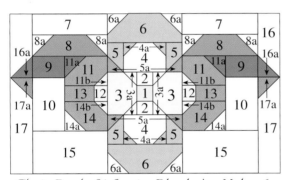

Chair Back & Seat. Block A. Make 6

correct placement of mirror image units 5, 11, 14, 16, and 17.

3. To assemble Block A, begin in the center of the block and join Unit 3 to opposite sides of the strip set units 1 and 2. Join mirror image Units 5 to opposite sides of Unit 4 as shown; then join Unit 6 to combined units 4-5 as shown.

4. Join units 7 and 8. Join units 9 and 10. Join units 12 and 13. Add mirror image Unit 11 to top of combined units 12-13 and mirror image Unit 14 to the bottom. Join combined units 9-10 to sides of combined units 11-12-13, referring to diagram frequently for correct placement of mirror image units. Carefully match the Unit 9 and 11 seams. Join combined units 7-8 to top of combined units 9-14; then add Unit 15 to bottom. Join this combination of units to opposite sides of flower center. Join mirror image units 16 and 17 in a vertical row. Make two and join to opposite ends of flower to complete Block A.

## Assembly Of Chair Back

1. Refer to diagram at top right for correct placement of Flower Block A. Join small border Q2, Block A, Unit Q1, Block A, and another border Q2 in a row as shown. Join small border Q3 to opposite sides of floral back. Join border Q4 to top and bottom; then add border Q5 to opposite sides.

## Assembly Of Chair Seat

1. For the seat, join Unit Q6 to opposite long sides of Block A. Join Unit Q7 border to opposite sides of floral seat; then join Unit

Q8 to top and bottom.

## Finishing

1. We used three layers of batting when the seats and back were quilted. Faye "ditched" the patchwork and did echo quilting around the flowers.

2. Make continuous straight-grain binding from 2 1/2" strips of Fabric V, and bind the back and the seat. To make the ties, cut 32" long lengths from the 1 1/2" strips of Fabric V. With right sides together, stitch the ties, leaving an opening to turn. Turn right side out and close the opening with a small piece of Steam-A-Seam 2. Top stitch along each edge and across the bottom of each strip. Stitch the ties on the back side of the seat by finding the center, and stitching down the center to hold them firmly in place.

3. For the bow, join two of the 8 1/2" x 25 1/2" strips together. Make four. Refer to illustration below and fold the bow in half lengthwise with right sides together. Trim corners on a 45° angle as shown above. Stitch around the bow as illustrated, leaving an opening to turn. Turn right side out and close opening with a small strip of Steam-A-Seam 2. Press the bow.

4. Fold the bow in the center in thirds. Stitch to the back side of the chair back down the center, pinning the folds so that they stay in place while stitching.

We had some fun with accessory items in the kitchen. We used purchased patterns for the tea cozy and valances, and created the towel using the Teapot Block and some cute lace

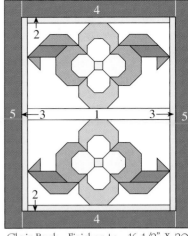

Chair Back. Finishes to: 16 1/2" X 20"

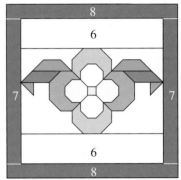

Chair Seat. Finishes to: 15" X 15 1/4"

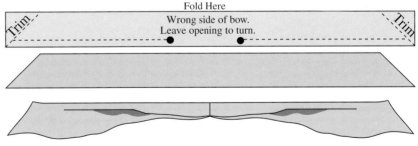

Fold Here
Wrong side of bow.
Leave opening to turn.
Trim
Trim

trim. The blocks are very versatile and may be used for so many attractive items.

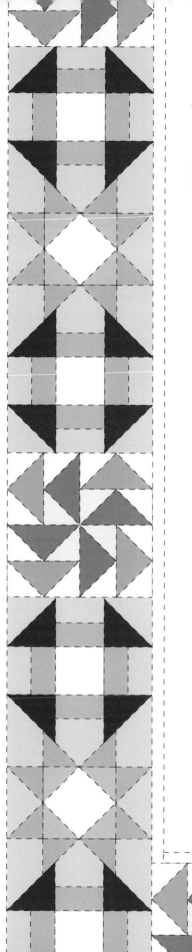

# A Patchwork Lunch

## For The Quilting Bunch

When we were preparing this luncheon (which we ate, by the way) Gigi came up with the fun idea of buying different colored breads, spreading them with the sandwich spreads, and cutting them into simple quilt blocks using the different colored breads in place of fabrics. She cut an Ohio Star, a Log Cabin, a Churn Dash and Flying Geese. Everyone enjoyed this spark of creativity! The sandwich spreads throughout the instruction pages are delicious and give a great variety. Enjoy!

## Zesty Chicken Spread

### Ingredients
1 - 12 oz. can of white chicken chunks, drained.
2/3 cup sour cream
1/2 cup canned chopped pineapple
1/2 teaspoon curry powder
1/2 cup chopped celery
1/4 cup currants

### Instructions
Mix all ingredients together and spread on sandwiches, crackers or fresh vegetables.

## Deviled Ham Delight

### Ingredients
1 can of deviled ham
1 teaspoon pickle relish
2 teaspoons mayonnaise

### Instructions
Mix ingredients and spread on sandwiches.

# Carolina Lily

## MATERIALS FOR ONE PLACE MAT

| | | | |
|---|---|---|---|
| ☐ | Fabric I (white with green print) | Need 9 1/2" | 3/8 yard |
| ■ | Fabric II (pink & green floral print) | Need 10 3/4" | 3/8 yard |
| ■ | Fabric III (pink print) | Need 12 1/2" | 1/2 yard |
| ■ | Fabric IV (dark rose print) | Need 12 1/2" | 1/2 yard |
| ■ | Fabric VI (dark olive print) | Need 6" | 1/4 yard |
| ■ | Fabric VII (light olive print) | Need 1 7/8" | 1/8 yard |
| | Backing | Need 14" x 18" | |

**CAROLINA LILY PLACE MAT.**
Finishes to: 14" x 18"
Quick pieced.

## CUTTING

☐ **From Fabric I, cut: (white with green print)**
- One 7 1/2" x 42" strip. From this, cut:
  * One - 5" x 7 1/2" (1)
  * One - 6 1/2" x 7" (16)
  * One - 5" x 7" (6)
  * One - 1 1/2" x 7" (7)
  * Two - 3 3/4" squares (4) stack this cut
  * Two - 3 1/2" squares (20c) stack this cut
  * Two - 3" x 3 1/2" (15a) stack this cut
  * Four - 2 7/8" squares (12, 13) stack this cut
  * Eight - 2 1/2" squares (18b, 18c, 20a) stack this cut
- One 2" x 42" strip. From this, cut:
  * One - 2" x 5" (5)
  * Two - 1 7/8" x 3 1/4" (8)
  * Four - 1 1/8" x 1 7/8" (9)
  * Four - 1 1/2" squares (18a, 20b)

■ **From Fabric II, cut: (pink and green floral print)**
- One 3 3/4" x 42" strip. From this, cut:
  * One - 3 3/4" x 7 1/2" (lily pocket lining)
  * One - 2 3/8" x 7 1/2" (2)
  * Two - 1 1/2" x 4 1/2" (10)
- Two 3 1/2" x 42" strips for straight-grain binding.

■ **From Fabric III, cut: (pink print)**
- One 12 1/2" x 42" strip. From this, cut:
  * One - 12 1/2" square for napkin
  * One - 3 1/2" square (17)
  * Eight - 2 1/2" x 3 1/2" (19)
  * Four - 1 7/8" squares (8a)

■ **From Fabric IV, cut: (dark rose print)**
- One 12 1/2" x 42" strip. From this, cut:
  * One - 12 1/2" square for napkin
  * Two - 3 1/2" squares (20)
  * Two - 2 1/2" x 3 1/2" (18)
  * One - 3" x 7 1/2" (15)

■ **From Fabric V, cut: (dark olive print)**
- One 3 1/2" x 42" strip. From this, cut:
  * One - 3 1/2" square (17c)
  * Fifteen - 2 1/2" squares (17a, 19b, 19c)

- One 2 1/2" x 42" strip. From this, cut:
  * Three - 2 1/2" squares (add to 2 1/2" sq. above)
  * Seventeen - 1 1/2" squares (17b, 19a)
  * Two - 2" squares (12a)
  * One - 1" x 4 1/2" (14)

■ **From Fabric VI, cut: (light olive print)**
- One 1 7/8" x 42" strip. From this, cut:
  * One - 1 7/8" x 7 1/2" (3)
  * Two - 1 7/8" x 4 1/2" (11)

## ASSEMBLY

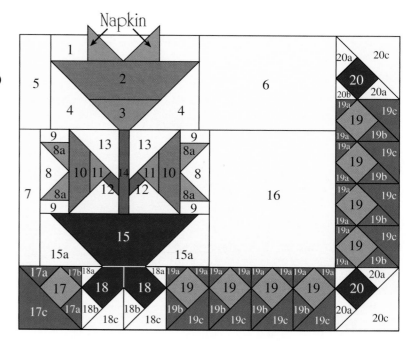

1. The illustration above is for construction of the entire place mat. Individual sections will be broken down. To begin, use diagonal corner technique to make eight of Unit 19. Add diagonal corners in alphabetical order. Make two of Unit 8, 18, and 20, and one of units 15 and 17.

2. Refer to illustration on following page for construction of the

pocket. To begin, join units 2 and 3. Use diagonal corner technique to join Unit 4 as shown. Place the pocket lining right sides

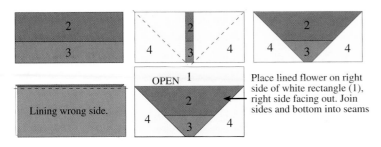

Place lined flower on right side of white rectangle (1), right side facing out. Join sides and bottom into seams

together on top of the flower and stitch across the top. Turn lining to inside and press. Follow instructions above for preparing the pocket.

3. To make the side flowers, refer to illustration below and begin

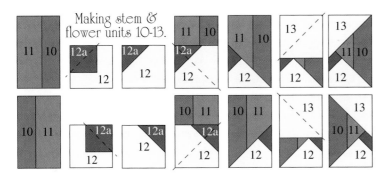

by joining units 10 and 11. Use diagonal corner technique to make Unit 12. Keep in mind that bottom drawings are mirror images of top drawings.

4. Unit 12 will now be used as a diagonal corner. Place Unit 12 on combined 10-11 units as shown, right sides together. Stitch the diagonal line, trim seam and press towards corner as shown. Join diagonal corner Unit 13 to top of combined units to complete the flower.

5. For corner units 17 and 20, the diagram below shows how to add the diagonal corners in alphabetical order. This is very important in the construction of this unit.

Corner Units 17 and 20.

6. To construct the place mat, begin by joining Unit 5 to left side of pocket unit and Unit 6 to right side of this combined unit. Be sure that your pocket and lining are pinned securely on Unit 1 as adding these seams will close the sides of the pocket.

7. Join Unit 9 to opposite short ends of Unit 8. Add these combined units to combined 10-13 flower units. Join these combined units to opposite sides of Unit 14 stem. Join Unit 15 to bottom; then add Unit 7 to left side. Join Unit 16 to right side as shown. Join this completed section to large flower section, matching stem Unit 14 to Unit 3. This will close the pocket.

8. Refer to bottom of place mat, and make a row beginning on the bottom left of Unit 17, two of Unit 18, and four of Unit 19. Join this row to bottom of place mat. For the right side of the place mat, beginning at the top right corner, make a vertical row by joining Unit 20 to opposite ends of four joined Units 19. Check place

mat diagram for correct placement of Unit 20. Join to place mat side.

**Finishing**
1. Refer to page 8 for making the frame binding and bind the place mat with the two joined 3 1/2" strips of Fabric II.
2. Refer to page 11 for making reversible napkin and make the napkin. Napkin folding is shown below. Fold the napkin and place it in the pocket.

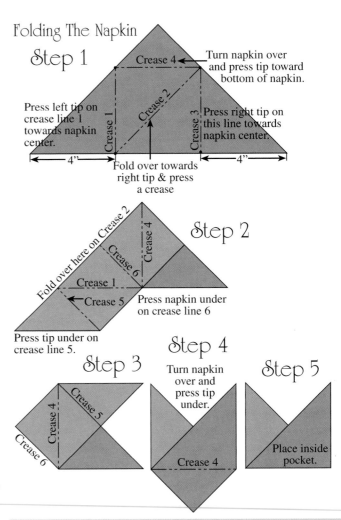

Folding The Napkin

Peanut Butter, Banana & Date Spread

*Ingredients*
1/2 cup smooth peanut butter
3 tablespoons honey
8 chopped, pitted dates
2 ripe bananas, mashed

*Instructions*

*Mix all ingredients well and use as a spread for sandwiches.*

59

# Churn Dash

## MATERIALS FOR ONE PLACE MAT

| |  | | | |
|---|---|---|---|---|
| ▫ | Fabric I (light tan print) | Need 9" | 3/8 yard |
| ■ | Fabric II (dark grape print) | Need 10 7/8" | 3/8 yard |
| ▨ | Fabric III (medium grape print) | Need 3 1/2" | 1/4 yard |
| ▥ | Fabric IV (dark grape check) | Need 12 1/2" | 1/2 yard |
| | Backing | Need 14" x 18" | |

## CUTTING

▫ **From Fabric I, cut: (light tan print)**
- One 5 1/2" x 42" strip. From this, cut:
  - * One - 5 1/2" x 10 1/2" (8)
  - * Two - 3 7/8" squares (Triangle squares 6)
  - * One - 3 1/2" x 9 1/2" (7)
  - * One - 3 1/2" x 6 1/2" (3)
  - * One - 3 1/2" square (1)
- One 3 1/2" x 42" strip. From this, cut:
  - * Three - 2" x 3 1/2" (5)
  - * One - 2 1/2" square (12b)
  - * Seven - 1 1/2" x 2 1/2" (11) Stack this cut.
  - * Eighteen - 1 1/2" sq. (6b, 9a, 10a, 12a) Stack this cut.

■ **From Fabric II, cut: (dark grape print)**
- One 3 7/8" x 42" strip. From this, cut:
  - * Two - 3 7/8" squares (Triangle squares 6)
  - * Two - 1 1/4" x 16 1/2" (13)
  - * Two - 1 1/4" x 14" (14)
- Two 3 1/2" x 42" strips for straight grain binding.

▨ **From Fabric III, cut: (medium grape print)**
- One 3 1/2" x 42" strip. From this, cut:
  - * One 3 1/2" x 6 1/2" (2)
  - * Three - 2" x 3 1/2" (4)
  - * Two - 2 1/2" squares (6a, 12)
  - * Eight - 1 1/2" x 2 1/2" (9, 10) Stack this cut.
  - * Fourteen - 1 1/2" squares (11a) Stack this cut.

▥ **From Fabric IV, cut: (dark grape check)**
- Two 12 1/2" squares for napkin.

## ASSEMBLY

**1.** Refer to page 9 for instructions on making triangle-squares with The Angler 2. Use 3 7/8" squares of Fabric I and II and make four triangle-squares for Unit 6.

**2.** Refer to illustration of place mat and use diagonal corner technique to make seven each of units 10 and 11. Make one each of Unit 6, 9, and 12.

**3.** Using drawings of pocket as a guide, join the units shown together to make the pocket. Follow the diagrams and instructions.

**4.** To assemble the place mat, begin by joining units 4 and 5 as shown. Make three. Join the diagonal corners on bottom right, Unit 6 triangle-square. Referring to diagram for correct placement, join Unit 6 to top and bottom of combined side units 4-5. Join remaining 4-5 units to bottom of pocket. This will close the bottom of the pocket. Join the combined 4-5-6 units to left side of place mat as shown; then add the remaining 4-5-6 units to right side. Join Unit 7 to top. Refer to bottom of place mat, and join

### CHURN DASH PLACE MAT. Finishes to: 14" x 18". Quick pieced.

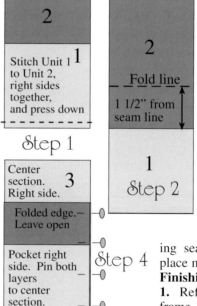

**Step 1** — **2** Stitch Unit 1 to Unit 2, right sides together, and press down **1**

**Step 2** — **2** Fold line / 1 1/2" from seam line / **1**

**Step 3** — Folded wrong sides together / Right side

**Step 4** — Center section. Right side. **3** / Folded edge.—Leave open / Pocket right side. Pin both layers to center section.

units 10 and 11, forming a zig zag design; then join Unit 9 to left side as shown. Add to bottom of Unit 8. Join to right side of Churn Dash, matching zig zag seams.

**5.** For right side, make five sets of joined 10-11 units as shown; then add Unit 12 to bottom matching seams. Add to right side of place mat as shown.

**Finishing**

**1.** Refer to page 8 for making the frame binding and bind the place mat with the two joined 3 1/2" strips of Fabric II.

**2.** Refer to page 11 for making reversible napkin and make the napkin. Fold the napkin and place it in the pocket.

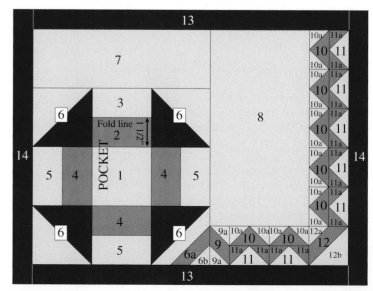

# Tulip

## MATERIALS FOR ONE PLACE MAT

| | | | |
|---|---|---|---|
| | Fabric I (tan on ivory print) | Need 8 1/4" | 1/2 yard |
| | Fabric II (dark red print) | Need 4 3/4" | 1/4 yard |
| | Fabric III (bright red print) | Need 4 3/4" | 1/4 yard |
| | Fabric IV (light olive print) | Need 4 1/2" | 1/4 yard |
| | Fabric V (dark olive print) | Need 10" | 3/8 yard |
| | Fabric VI (gold print) | Need 12 1/2" | 1/2 yard |
| | Backing | Need 14" x 18" | |

## CUTTING

**From Fabric I, cut: (tan on ivory print)**
- One 4 3/4" x 42" strip. From this, cut:
  * One - 4 3/4" square (2)
  * Two - 2 3/8" x 4 3/4" (1)
  * Two - 1 1/4" x 4 3/4" (5)
  * Two - 4 1/2" squares (8c)
  * One - 3 5/8" x 18 1/2" (11)
- One 3 1/2" x 42" strip. From this, cut:
  * Two - 3 1/2" squares (8a)
  * Four - 3" x 3 1/2" (9a, 10a)
  * Four - 3" squares (9c, 10c)
  * Four - 2 5/8" squares (6a, 7a)

**From Fabric II, cut: (dark red print)**
- One 4 3/4" x 42" strip. From this, cut:
  * Three - 4 3/4" squares (4, 6b, 7c)
  * Four - 2 5/8" squares (8b, 9b)

**From Fabric III, cut: (bright red print)**
- One 4 3/4" x 42" strip. From this, cut:
  * Three - 4 3/4" squares (3, 6c, 7b)
  * Two - 2 5/8" squares (10b)

**From Fabric IV, cut: (light olive print)**
- One 4 1/2" x 42" strip. From this, cut:
  * Two - 4 1/2" x 5 7/8" (8)
  * Two - 3" x 5 3/8" (9)
  * Two - 3" squares (10c)
  * Two - 1 1/2" squares (1a)

**From Fabric V, cut: (dark olive print)**
- One 3" x 42" strip. From this, cut:
  * Two - 3" x 5 3/8" (10)
  * Four - 3" squares (8d, 9c)
  * One - 1 1/4" x 18 1/2" (12)
- Two 3 1/2" x 42" strips for straight-grain binding.

**From Fabric VI, cut: (gold print)**
- One 12 1/2" x 42" strip. From this, cut:
  * Two - 12 1/2" squares for napkins
  * Two - 4 3/4" squares (6, 7)

## ASSEMBLY

**1.** The diagonal corner technique will be used on this project, however we have illustrated how we have used it as many of the units are "built" using this technique, along with the diagonal end technique and triangle-squares shown on page 7. When assembling the units, refer to the illustration below of the complete place mat.

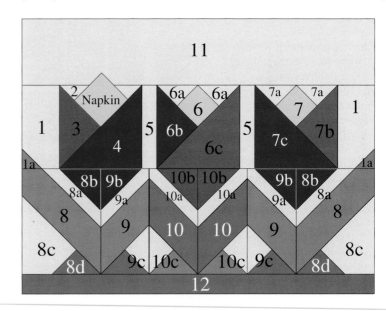

**2.** To begin, refer to the diagram below for making units 6 and 7 as they are both made in the same way. Join diagonal corners in alphabetical order as shown for the tulip top.

Making mirror image units 6 and 7.

**3.** To make the pocket, shown below right, fold the 4 3/4" squares of fabrics II and III in half diagonally. Place them as shown in the drawing. Pin them securely in place to avoid shifting. They will be sewn into seams later, leaving the pocket for the napkin.

**4.** Refer to the diagrams and instructions in the gold box on the following page for directions on making triangle-squares 9c and 10c. Please note

Pocket

61

that you will be making two, however, they are mirror images. Check the illustration of the place mat for correct placement.

**Step 1**

**Step 2**

Use this assembly for units 9c & 10c.
1. For Unit 9c, place 3" squares of fabrics I and V right sides together, matching raw edges, and stitch a diagonal line down the center as shown. Press open and trim center seam, leaving the top and base fabric.

2. For Unit 10c, place 3" squares of fabrics I & IV right sides together and stitch a diagonal line as before. Press open and trim center seam, leaving the top and base fabric.

**5.** To assemble Unit 8, refer to the illustration for making mirror image Unit 8 at right. First use diagonal corner technique to make Unit 8c. This unit now becomes the diagonal corner at the bottom of Unit 8. Place the 8c unit as shown on Unit 8. Stitch the diagonal, trim seam and press downwards. To complete Unit 8, join diagonal corner units 8a and 8b in alphabetical order. Check place mat diagram for correct placement of these units as they are mirror images.

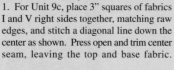

Making mirror image Unit 8

**6.** To make mirror image Unit 9, refer to diagram at right and begin by joining diagonal end 9a. Trim seam and press unit upwards. Join Unit 9c, following the diagram. This is the triangle-square unit previously

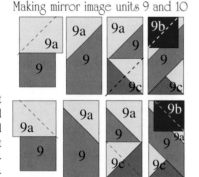

Making mirror image units 9 and 10

made. Stitch the diagonal, trim seam and press downwards. Join diagonal corner 9b to complete the unit. Unit 10 is made the same way, except for the color differences.

**7.** Use diagonal corner technique to make mirror image Unit 1. To assemble the place mat, begin by joining Unit 1 to left side of pocket section, and Unit 5 to right side, closing in the pocket sides in the seams. Join another Unit 5 to right side of Unit 6; then add Unit 7 to Unit 5 as shown. Complete the row by joining Unit 1 to right side. Join Unit 11 across the top of the tulip top row.

**8.** For the bottom section, refer to diagram of place mat on Page 61 for correct placement of mirror image units. Join Unit 8, Unit 9, the two mirror image units 10, mirror image Unit 9, and mirror image Unit 8. Join Unit 12 across the bottom as shown. Join the leaf bottom to the tulip top, matching all seams carefully to complete the place mat.

**Finishing**

**1.** Refer to page 8 for making the frame binding and bind the place mat with the two joined 3 1/2" strips of Fabric V.
**2.** Refer to page 11 for making reversible napkin and make the napkin. Fold the napkin and place it in the pocket.

# DUTCHMAN'S PUZZLE

DUTCHMAN'S PUZZLE PLACE MAT.
Finishes to: 14" x 18". Quick pieced.

## MATERIALS FOR ONE PLACE MAT

| | | |
|---|---|---|
| ☐ | Fabric I (pale green print) 3/8 yard | Need 9 1/2" |
| ☐ | Fabric II (med.. green print) 1/8 yard | Need 2" |
| ☐ | Fabric III (dark green print) 1/2 yard | Need 12 1/2" |
| ☐ | Fabric IV (dark purple print) 3/8 yard | Need 11 1/2" |
| ☐ | Fabric V (medium purple print) 1/2 yard | Need 12 1/2" |
| ☐ | Fabric VI (light lavender print) 1/8 yard | Need 2" |
| ☐ | Fabric VII (bright yellow print) 1/8 yard | Need 2" |
| ☐ | Fabric VIII (light yellow print) 1/8 yard | Need 2" |
| | Backing | Need 14 1/2" x 18 1/2" |

## CUTTING

☐ **From Fabric I, cut: (pale green print)**
• One 9 1/2" x 42" strip. From this, cut:
    * One - 9 1/2" x 11" (1)
    * One - 3 1/2" x 6 1/2" (7)
    * Twelve - 2" squares (4a, 5a, 6a)

☐ **From Fabric II, cut: (medium green print)**
• One 2" x 42" strip. From this, cut:
    * Ten - 2" squares (2a, 3a)

☐ **From Fabric III, cut: (dark green print)**
• One 12 1/2" x 42" strip. From this, cut:
    * One - 12 1/2" square for napkin
    * Two - 3 1/2" x 6 1/2" for pocket lining and pocket back
    * Twelve - 2" squares (8a, 9a)

**From Fabric IV, cut:  (dark purple print)**
- Two 3 1/2" x 42" strips for straight-grain binding.
- One 2" x 42" strip. From this, cut:
  - * Four - 2" x 3 1/2" (8)
- Two 1 1/4" x 42" strips. From these, cut:
  - * Two - 1 1/4" x 17" (10)
  - * Two - 1 1/4" x 14" (11)

**From Fabric V, cut:  (medium purple print)**
- One 12 1/2" x 42" strip. From this, cut:
  - * One - 12 1/2" square for napkin
  - * Seven - 2" x 3 1/2" (2, 9)

**From Fabric VI, cut:  (light lavender print)**
- One 2" x 42" strip. From this, cut:
  - * Four - 2" x 3 1/2" (3, 4)

**From Fabric VII, cut:  (bright yellow print)**
- One 2" x 42" strip. From this, cut:
  - * One - 2" x 3 1/2" (5)
  - * Four - 2" squares (8b)

**From Fabric VIII, cut:  (light yellow print)**
- One 2" x 42" strip. From this, cut:
  - * Three - 2" x 3 1/2" (6)

## ASSEMBLY

**1.**  All of the blocks in this place mat are flying geese blocks. Refer to page 9 for making the blocks with The Angler 2. Use diagonal corner technique to make all of the flying geese blocks.

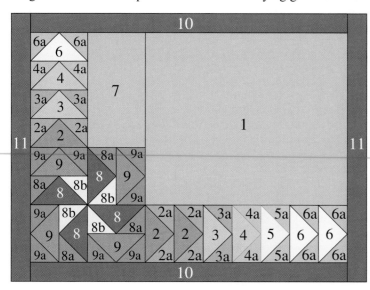

**2.**  Refer to the diagram at right for making the pocket. Join the 8 and 9 units together as shown. Place the pocket lining right sides together on the joined units, and stitch across the top as shown. Turn lining to the inside and press. The pocket will be sewn into the right side seam and bound into the place mat on the left side and the bottom. The top is left open. Begin by joining units 6, 4, 3,2, and pocket back in a vertical row. Pin the pocket on top of the pocket back so that it

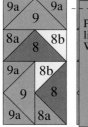

will be sewn into the seams and left open at the top.  Join units 8 and 9 together.  Make two.  Refer to place mat diagram, and join the two  combined 8-9 units as shown; then add Unit 7 to the top. For the flying geese row across the bottom of the place mat, from left to right, join two of Unit 2, Unit 3, Unit 4, Unit 5, and two of Unit 6 as shown.  Join Unit 1 to top of flying geese blocks.

**3.**  Join the three pieced sections together to complete the place mat top.

### Finishing
**1.**  Refer to page 8 for making the frame binding and bind the place mat with the two joined 3 1/2" strips of Fabric IV.
**2.**  Refer to page 11 for making reversible napkin and make the napkin.  Fold the napkin and place it in the pocket.

Hawaiian Ham Spread

*Ingredients*
1 1/2 cups cooked, ground ham (ham may be ground in a food processor)
1 - 8 oz. can crushed pineapple drained
1 teaspoon packed brown sugar
1/8 teaspoon ground cloves
1 1/2 tablespoons mayonnaise

*Instructions*
Combine all ingredients and stir well.

Pam's Blender Salad Dressing

*Ingredients*
1 chopped medium onion
3 stalks of celery
3 raw eggs
1 tablespoon black pepper
1/4 teaspoon dry mustard
1 tablespoon Accent
1 large garlic clove
2 cups of oil
1 small can anchovies

*Instructions*
Place all ingredients in a blender and mix thoroughly - until smooth.  Chill for about an hour.

**This is a wonderful salad dressing served freshly made.  It will keep in the refrigerator for 2-3 days.  Do not keep any longer.

# Ohio Star

## MATERIALS FOR ONE PLACE MAT

| | | | |
|---|---|---|---|
| ■ | Fabric I (navy print) | Need 11 1/4" | 3/8 yard |
| □ | Fabric II (light tan print) | Need 6 1/4" | 1/4 yard |
| ▨ | Fabric III (medium blue print) | Need 12 1/2" | 1/2 yard |
| ▨ | Fabric IV (medium tan print) | Need 9" | 3/8 yard |
| | Backing | Need 14" x 18" | |

## CUTTING

**From Fabric I, cut: (navy print)**
- One 11 1/4" x 42" strip. From this, cut:
  * One - 11 1/4" x 11 3/4" (1)
  * One - 3 1/2" square (7)
  * One - 2 3/4" x 3 1/2" (5)
  * Three - 2" x 3 1/2" (3)
  * One - 2" x 2 3/4" (2)

**From Fabric II, cut: (light tan print)**
- One 3 1/2" x 42" strip. From this, cut:
  * Two - 3 1/2" x 6 1/2" (pocket lining and pocket back)
  * Two - 3 1/2" squares (6)
  * Four - 2 3/4" x 3 1/2" (8)
- One 2 3/4" x 42" strip. From this, cut:
  * One - 2 3/4" x 12 3/4" (4)
  * Two - 2 3/4" squares (9)

**From Fabric III, cut: (medium blue print)**
- One 12 1/2" x 42" strip. From this, cut:
  * Two - 12 1/2" squares for napkin.
  * Sixteen - 2" squares (3a, 5a, 7a, 8a)

**From Fabric IV, cut: (medium tan print)**
- Two 3 1/2" x 42" strips for straight-grain binding.
- One 2" x 42" strip. From this, cut:
  * Eight - 2" squares (6a)

## ASSEMBLY

1. Use diagonal corner technique to make three of Unit 8, two each of unit 3, and 6, and one each of units 5 and 7. Refer to illustration of pocket,

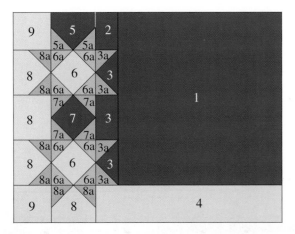

## OHIO STAR PLACE MAT.
Finishes to: 14" x 18". Quick pieced.

and join units 6 and 7 as shown. Place the pocket lining right sides together on the joined units, and stitch across the top as shown. Turn lining to the inside and press. The pocket will be sewn into the seams. The top is left open.

2. To assemble the place mat, begin on the left side. Join the three Unit 8's together. Refer to place mat illustration of this section, as two of the units have 8a diagonal corners and one does not. Join Unit 9 to opposite ends of the joined Unit 8's.

3. For star center row, join Unit 5 and pocket back. Pin the pocket on top of the pocket back; then join Unit 6 to the bottom of the pocket which will close the seam at the bottom of the pocket. Add remaining Unit 8 to bottom of Unit 6.

4. Join three of Unit 3 together. Refer to place mat illustrations of this section, as two of the units have 3a diagonal corners and one does not. Join Unit 2 to top of the row; then add Unit 1 to right side. Join Unit 4 to bottom.

5. Join the three rows together. The pocket will now be sewn into the side seams, leaving the top open for the napkin.

**Finishing**

1. Refer to page 8 for making the frame binding and bind the place mat with the two joined 3 1/2" strips of Fabric IV.

2. Refer to page 11 for making reversible napkin and make the napkin. Fold the napkin and place it in the pocket.

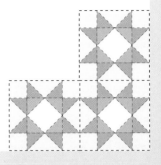

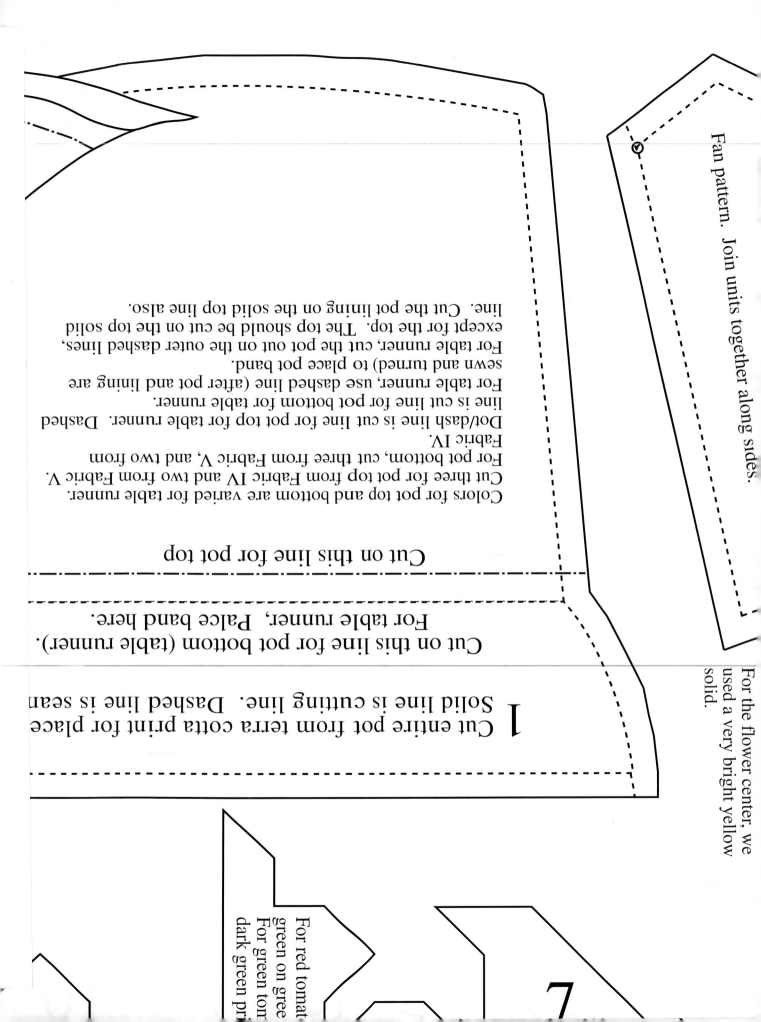

Fan pattern. Join units together along sides.

For the flower center, we used a very bright yellow solid.

Cut on this line for pot top

Colors for pot top and bottom are varied for table runner.
Cut three for pot top from Fabric IV and two from Fabric V.
For pot bottom, cut three from Fabric V, and two from Fabric IV.
Dot/dash line is cut line for pot top for table runner. Dashed line is cut line for pot bottom for table runner.
For table runner, use dashed line (after pot and lining are sewn and turned) to place pot band.
For table runner, cut the pot out on the outer dashed lines, except for the top. The top should be cut on the top solid line. Cut the pot lining on the solid top line also.

Cut on this line for pot bottom (table runner).
For table runner. Palce band here.

1 Cut entire pot from terra cotta print for place...
Solid line is cutting line. Dashed line is seam...

For red tomat...
green on gree...
For green tom...
dark green pri...

7

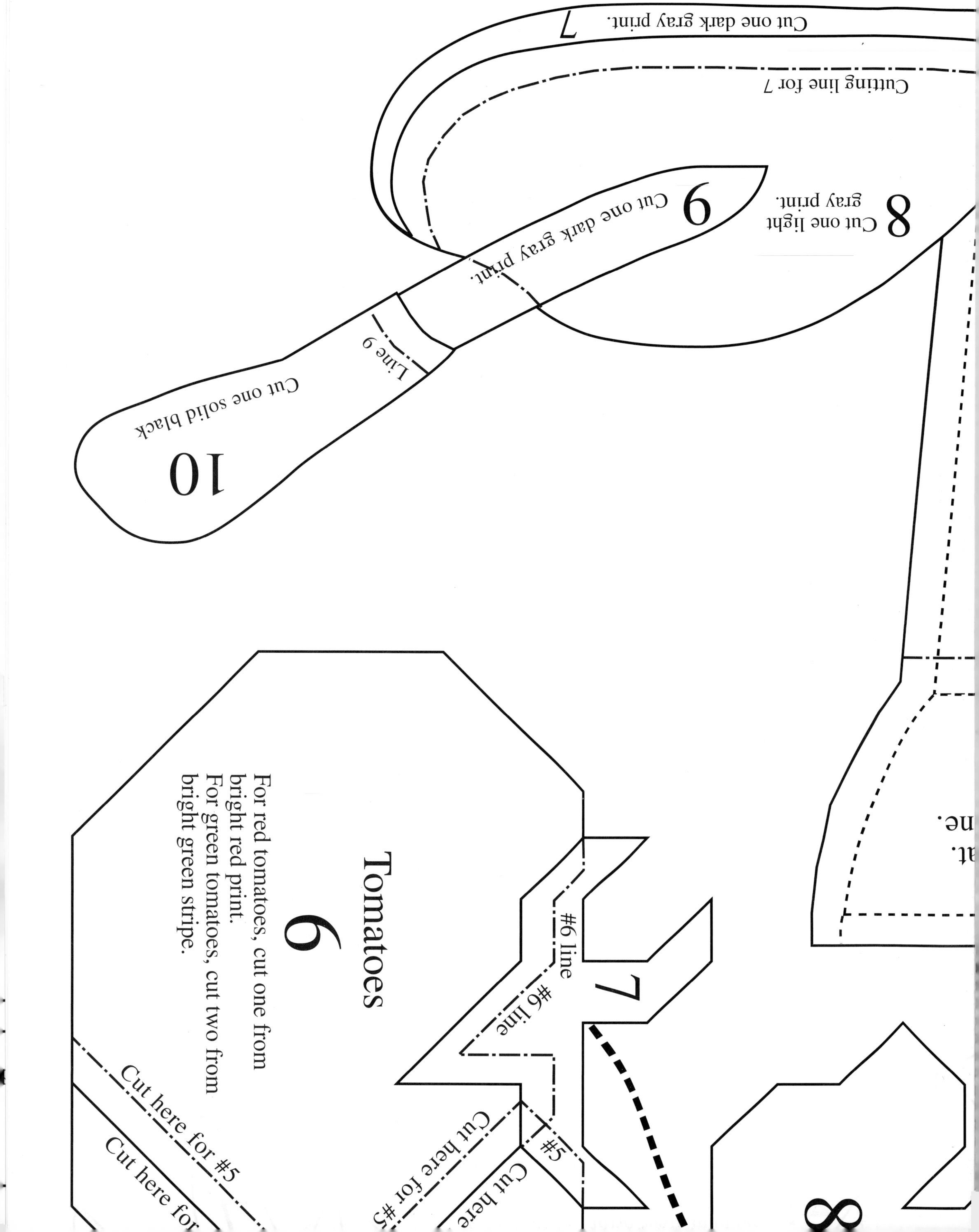

Cut one dark gray print.

7

Cutting line for 7

8 Cut one light
gray print.

9 Cut one dark gray print.

Line 9

10 Cut one solid black

Tomatoes
6

For red tomatoes, cut one from
bright red print.
For green tomatoes, cut two from
bright green stripe.

#6 line

#6 line

7

#5

8

Cut here for #5

Cut here for #5

Cut here for #5

Cut here for

# LOG CABIN

## MATERIALS FOR ONE PLACE MAT

LOG CABIN PLACE MAT.
Finishes to: 14" x 18". Quick pieced.

| Fabric I (dk. green print) | Need 9 1/4" | 3/8 yard |
| Fabric II (yellow on ivory print) | Need 19 1/2" | 3/8 yard |
| Fabric III (brown and rust print) | Need 3 1/2" x 7 1/2" | scrap |
| Fabric IV (very dk. green print) | Need 3" x 7" | scrap |
| Fabric V (medium green print) | Need 2 1/2" x 7 1/2" | scrap |
| Fabric VI (dark brown print) | Need 2" x 7 1/2" | scrap |
| Fabric VII (dk. barn red print) | Need 13" x 14" | lg. scrap |
| Fabric VIII (medium gold print) | Need 2" x 7 1/2" | scrap |
| Fabric IX (light gold print) | Need 2 1/2" x 7 1/2" | scrap |
| Fabric X (dark gold print) | Need 3" x 7 1/2" | scrap |
| Backing and Batting | Need 14 3/4" x 18 1/4" | |

## CUTTING

**From Fabric I, cut: (dark green print)**
• One 9 1/4" x 42" strip. From this, cut:
   * One - 9 1/4" x 11" (1)
   * One - 5 3/4" square (5)
   * One - 2 1/4" x 7 1/2" (2)
   * Five - 2 5/8" squares (3) Cut in half diagonally

**From Fabric II, cut: (yellow on ivory print)**
• One 12 1/2" x 42" strip. From this, cut:
   * One - 12 1/2" square for napkin.
   * One - 6" square for pocket lining.
   * One - 4 3/8" square (6) Cut in half diagonally
   * Six - 2 5/8" squares (4) Cut in half diagonally.
   * Seven 1" squares (A1)
   * Two 3 1/2" x 42" strips for straight-grain binding.

**From Fabric III, cut: (brown and rust print)**
• Seven - 1" x 3" (A9)

**From Fabric IV, cut: (very dk. green print)**
• Seven - 1" x 2 1/2" (A8)

**From Fabric V, cut: (medium green print)**
• Seven - 1" x 2" (A5)

**From Fabric VI, cut: (dark brown print)**
• Seven - 1" x 1 1/2" (A4)

**From Fabric VII, cut: (dark barn red print)**
• One 12 1/2" square for napkin
   * Seven - 1" squares (A2)

**From Fabric VIII, cut: (medium gold print)**
• Seven - 1" x 1 1/2" (A3)

**From Fabric IX, cut: (light gold print)**
• Seven - 1" x 2" (A6)

**From Fabric X, cut: (dark gold print)**
• Seven - 1" x 2 1/2" (A7)

## ASSEMBLY

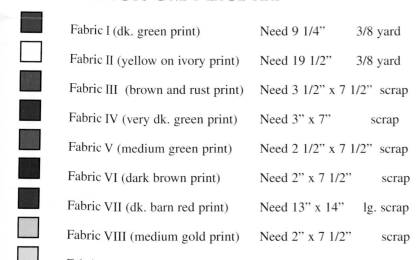

Extend backing and batting 1" beyond top before binding.

**1.** To assemble the place mat, make the log cabin, Block A at right. Begin in the center and join each new piece in numerical order. It is critical on this design that seam allowances are consistent. We suggest using a "scant" 1/4" seam throughout. Make seven of Block A.

Block A. Make 7
Finishes to 3 1/2" sq.

**2.** Block A will be turned "on point" and triangles added to each block. Begin by joining triangle #3 to opposite ends of five log cabin blocks. Press seams towards dark. Join Unit 4 triangles to remaining ends of the five blocks.

**3.** For the pocket, refer to the place mat diagram above and join two of the log cabin blocks as shown. Join Unit 4 triangles to opposite ends of the two A blocks; then add triangle 6 to the bottom of the joined blocks as shown.

**4.** Using the two log cabin blocks with joined triangles as a pattern, place right sides together on top of the 6" square of Fabric II and pin so that the fabrics stay together and don't shift. Cut out the lining. Stitch across the long diagonal edge as shown. Turn pocket lining to the inside and press. Pin all raw edges together. They will be sewn into the seams later.

**5.** To assemble the place mat, refer to the place mat diagram, and join two of the singular log cabin blocks together. Join Unit 2 to right side of the blocks. Pin the pocket in place on top of Unit 5, right sides of Unit 5 facing up and right side of pocket facing up. Raw edges need to be even on left side and bottom. Pin them together to avoid shifting. Join Unit 5 with pocket to bottom of combined log cabin blocks and Unit 2.

**6.** Join the remaining three log cabin blocks as shown in diagram. Join Unit 1 to top. Join this section to pocket section, matching the tips of the log cabin blocks. This will secure the pocket on two short sides.

Wrong side of Fabric II

**Finishing**

**1.** Lay the batting on top of the 14 3/4" x 18 1/4" backing. Center the place mat on top of the batting. There should be 1" of backing and batting all around the place mat. Refer to page 8 for making the frame binding and bind the place mat with the two joined 3 1/2" strips of Fabric II. The batting and backing will fill the binding.

**2.** Refer to page 11 for making reversible napkin and make the napkin. The napkin fold is shown below.

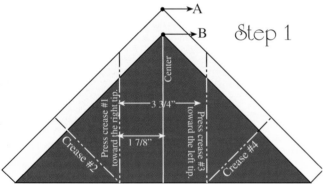

Fold and press napkin so that point B is 1 1/8" from point A.

## Step 1

## Step 2

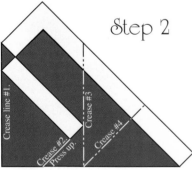

## Steps 3 & 4

# From the Earth

## Sicilian Vegetable Medley

### Ingredients
2 yellow squash with peel
2 medium size zucchinis with peel
1 small eggplant peeled
1 onion sliced
2 cloves of garlic minced
1 green bell pepper sliced
1 red bell pepper sliced
1 yellow bell pepper sliced
1 orange bell pepper sliced
2 tablespoons olive oil
1 - 16 oz. can diced tomatoes
1/2 teaspoon dried basil
2 teaspoons dried oregano
salt and pepper to taste
1/2 cup grated Parmesan cheese

### Instructions
Preheat oven to 325 degrees. In a large saute pan heat olive oil over medium heat. Add squash, eggplant, peppers, garlic and onion. Saute until all vegetables are soft. Add tomatoes with juice. Season with basil, oregano, salt and pepper until you reach desired taste.
Transfer ingredients to a glass baking dish. Bake for 20 minutes at 325. Sprinkle with Parmesan cheese and bake another 10 minutes.
Makes 6 servings.

## MATERIALS FOR TABLECLOTH

| | | | |
|---|---|---|---|
| ☐ | Fabric I (natural osnaburg) | Need 99" | 2 7/8 yards |
| ▦ | Fabric II (bright green plaid) | Need 31" | 1 yard |
| ☐ | Fabric III (bright yellow textured print) | Need 5" | 1/4 yard |
| ☐ | Fabric IV (bright yellow stripe) | Need 4 1/2" | 1/4 yard |
| ☐ | Fabric V (white Ultra Suede) | Need 14 1/2" x 18" | 1/2 yard |
| ■ | Fabric VI (dark purple marble print) | Need 11" | 3/8 yard |
| ■ | Fabric VII (bright purple print) | Need 8 3/4" | 3/8 yard |
| ■ | Fabric VIII (burgundy print) | Need 15 1/4" | 1/2 yard |
| ■ | Fabric IX (bright magenta print) | Need 1 1/2" | 3/8 yard |
| ■ | Fabric X (bright red print) | Need 11 3/4" | 3/8 yard |
| ■ | Fabric XI (dark red textured print) | Need 5 1/4" x 6" | scrap |
| ▨ | Fabric XII (bright orange marble print) | Need 13 1/2" | 1/2 yard |
| ■ | Fabric XIII (dk. green textured print) | Need 5 1/2" x 18" | 1/4 yard |
| ■ | Fabric XIV (medium green print) | Need 10 1/2" | 3/8 yard |
| ▤ | Fabric XV (bright green stripe) | Need 10" | 3/8 yard |
| ■ | Fabric XVI (solid bright med..green) | Need 5 1/2" | 1/4 yard |
| ▨ | Fabric XVII (dark green print) | Need 6 1/4" x 18" | 1/4 yard |
| ▨ | Fabric XVIII (green on green dot) | Need 8 1/2" x 18" | 3/8 yard |
| ▨ | Fabric XIX (med.. green marble print) | Need 8 3/4" x 18" | 3/8 yard |

18" wide Steam-A-Seam 2 and tear-away stabilizer    3 yards
Backing    3 5/8 yards

## CUTTING

All "Q" units in cutting instructions stand for tablecloth top. These units are not incorporated into the appliqué's, but are on the tablecloth top. Please read Step 1 under ASSEMBLY before cutting osnaburg.

*\* We have calculated the amount of fabric needed for the appliqués, and the pieces to be cut from the fabric sizes given are indicated with each cut. Appliqué pattern pieces are found on large pattern sheet.*

☐ **From Fabric I, cut: (natural osnaburg)**
- Four 13 1/2" x 42" strips. From these, cut:
  * Two - 13 1/2" x 23 1/2" background for tomatoes (4)
  * Two - 13 1/2" x 18" background for beets (3)
  * Two - 13 1/2" x 16 3/4" background for peppers (2)
  * Two - 13 1/2" x 15 3/4" background for eggplant (1)
- Ten 4 1/2" x 42" strips. From these, cut:
  * Forty - 4 1/2" squares (Q12)

▦ **From Fabric II, cut: (bright green plaid)**
- Six 2 1/2" x 42" strips for straight-grain binding.
- Eight 2" x 42" strips. From these, cut:
  * Eight - 2" x 24 1/2" (Q13)
  * Eight - 2" x 9 3/4" (Q6)

## FROM THE EARTH TABLECLOTH
### Finishes to: 60" Square.
### Quick pieced and appliqué.

☐ **From Fabric III, cut: (bright yellow textured print)**
- One 2" x 42" strip. From this, cut:
  * Sixteen - 2" squares (Q5)
- One 3" x 18" for appliqué yellow pepper #7, and twenty-eight flower centers.

☐ **From Fabric IV, cut: (bright yellow stripe)**
- One 4 1/2" x 42" strip. From this, cut:
  * Seven - 4 1/2" squares (Q9)
  * One 4 1/2" x 7" for yellow pepper #8 appliqué

☐ **From Fabric V, cut: (white Ultra Suede)**
*\* Ultra Suede may be substituted with a bright white cotton.*
- One 14 1/2" x 18" for 28 appliqué flowers.

■ **From Fabric VI, cut: (dark purple marble print)**
- One 4 1/2" x 42" strip. From this, cut:
  * Nine - 4 1/2" squares (Q10)
- One 6 1/2" x 18" for eggplant #5 appliqué .

■ **From Fabric VII, cut: (bright purple print)**
- One 4 1/2" x 42" strip. From this, cut:
  * Nine - 4 1/2" squares (Q10)
- One 4 1/4" x 18" for eggplant #4 appliqué .

■ **From Fabric VIII, cut: (burgundy print)**
- One 4 1/2" x 42" strip. From this, cut:
  * Eight - 4 1/2" squares (Q11)
- One 10 3/4" x 18" beet #5 and #7 appliqués

■ **From Fabric IX, cut: (bright magenta print)**
- One 4 1/2" x 42" strip. From this, cut:
  * Eight - 4 1/2" squares (Q11)
- One 7" x 11" beet #4 and #6 appliqués.

■ **From Fabric X, cut: (bright red print)**
- One 4 1/2" x 42" strip. From this, cut:
  * Nine - 4 1/2" squares (Q7)
- One 7 1/4" x 18" for pepper #4 and #7, and tomato #3 and #6 appliqués.

■ **From Fabric XI, cut: (dark red textured print)**
- One 5 1/4" x 6" for tomato #2 and #5 appliqués.

▨ **From Fabric XII, cut: (bright orange marble print)**
- Three 4 1/2" x 42" strips. From these, cut:
  * Sixteen - 4 1/2" squares (Q7, Q9)
- One - 4 1/2" x 18" for pepper #5 and #8 appliqués.

■ **From Fabric XIII, cut: (dark green textured print)**
- One 5 1/2" x 18" for tomato #4 and #7, pepper #6 and #9, and eggplant #3 appliqués.

■ **From Fabric XIV, cut: (medium green print)**
- One 4 1/2" x 42" strip. From this, cut:

* Eight - 4 1/2" squares (Q8)
• One 6" x 18" for eggplant #6, pepper leaves #1, #2, #3, and#7, and pepper #4 appliqués..

**From Fabric XV, cut: (bright green stripe)**
• One 4 1/2" x 42" strip. From this, cut:
  * Eight - 4 1/2" squares (Q8)
• One 5 1/2" x 11" for green tomato #3 and #6 appliqués.

**From Fabric XVI, cut: (solid bright medium green)**
• One 5 1/2" x 13" for pepper #5, and tomato #2 and #5 appliqués.

**From Fabric XVII, cut: (dark green print)**
• One 6 1/4" x 18" for green tomato #1 and #8, and beet #9 appliqués.

**From Fabric XVIII, cut: (green on green dot)**
• One 8 1/2" x 18" for red tomato #1 and #8, eggplant #2 and #7, and pepper #1, #2, #3, and #7 appliqués.

**From Fabric XIX, cut: (medium green marble print)**
• One 8 3/4" x 18" for beet #8 and eggplant #1 appliqués.

## ASSEMBLY

**1.** Refer to appliqué directions on page 11. All of the appliqués are on the large pattern sheet. Each vegetable appliqué is numbered and each appliqué should be placed on the osnaburg in numerical order. Patterns not only show where to cut, the dot/dashed lines show where pieces will overlap each other. Refer to the diagram below for placement of the vegetables on the osnaburg. The exact cut sizes are given for the osnaburg.

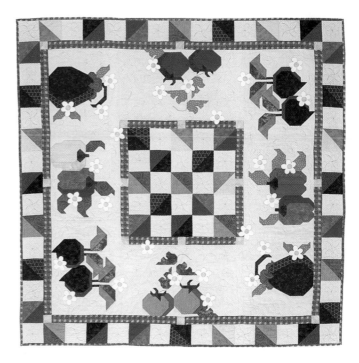

We suggest cutting it about 1" larger as each vegetable is placed 1/4" up from the bottom of the osnaburg so that the sashing strip seams will allow the vegetables to "sit on top" of them. If vegetables are placed 1" from bottom edge of osnaburg, when appliqué is complete, the osnaburg can be trimmed to the correct size.

**2.** We used a blanket stitch around all of the vegetables and flowers, with bright rayon thread colors. Before stitching, place tear-away stabilizer behind each appliqué and remove it when stitching is complete.

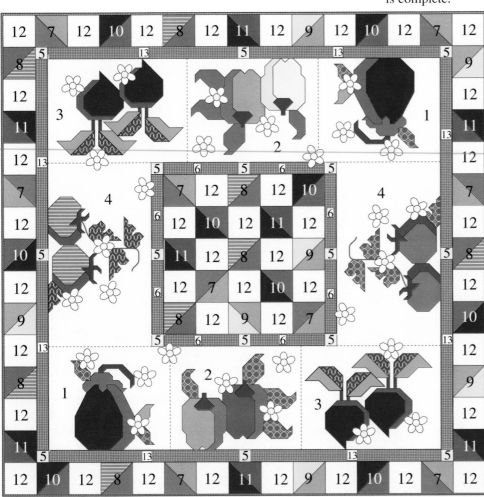

**3.** Refer to page 7 to make the triangle-squares. Use the different 4 1/2" squares to form the triangle-squares. Begin by making the center section first. Join the triangle-squares in rows as shown, alternating with the osnaburg squares. Join the rows together. Join all sashing strips #6 to opposite sides of #5 sashing square. Add to top and bottom of center section. Join #5 square to opposite ends of remaining sashing strips and join to opposite sides of center section. As a few of the white flowers overlap the sashing, add them now and appliqué in place.

**4.** Join the tomatoes to opposite sides of center section. Refer to diagram and join the other vegetables together as shown. Add them to top and bottom of center section.

**5.** Make the large sashing strips as you did in Step 3 and join them as directed. Using diagram as a guide, join the remaining triangle-squares together and join to tablecloth top.

### Finishing

**1.** Faye quilted leaves and small flowers swirling around the vegetables and in the #12 squares.

**2.** Use the six 2 1/2" wide strips of Fabric II, and make approximately 255" of straight-grain binding, and bind the tablecloth.

# Poinsettia

## MATERIALS

| | | | |
|---|---|---|---|
| ☐ | Fabric I  (white with gold print) | Need 25 1/8" | 3/4 yard |
| ▨ | Fabric II  (medium green print) | Need 25" | 3/4 yard |
| ▨ | Fabric III  (bright red print) | Need 7 1/2" | 1/4 yard |
| ■ | Fabric IV  (dark red print) | Need 16 1/4" | 5/8 yard |
| ▨ | Fabric V  (bright green print) | Need 6 1/4" | 1/4 yard |
| ▨ | Fabric VI  (gold lamé) | Need 1 3/4" | 1/8 yard |
| | Backing | Need 1 yard if backing is pieced. | |

All "Q" units in cutting instructions stand for table runner top. These are units that are not incorporated into the specific blocks, but are on the table runner top.

Because of the nature of this design, it is critical that your seams are very accurate on the A block. We suggest taking "scant" 1/4" seams to insure correct sizes.

## CUTTING

☐ **From Fabric I, cut:  (white with gold print)**
- One 8 1/2" x 42" strip. From this, cut:
  * Eight - 4 1/2 " x 8 1/2" (Q3)
  * One - 5 7/8" sq. (Q1)  Cut in half diagonally
- One 4 1/2 " x 42" strip. From this, cut:
  * Four - 4 1/2" sq. (Q4)  Cut in half diagonally.

- Cut remainder into five 1 1/8" strips.  From these and scrap, cut:
  * Sixty-four - 1 1/8" x 1 1/4" (A4)
- Three 1 7/8" x 42" strips. From these, cut:
  * Sixty-four - 1 7/8" squares (A6)
- Four 1 1/8" x 42" strips. From these and scrap, cut:
  * 128 - 1 1/8" squares (A2b)
- Two 1" x 42" strips. From these, cut:
  * Sixty-four - 1" squares (A8a, A9)

▨ **From Fabric II, cut:  (medium green print)**
- One 8 1/2" x 42" strip. From this, cut:
  * Eight - 4 1/2" x 8 1/2" (Q3)
- One 4 1/2" x 42" strip. From this, cut:
  * Two - 4 1/2" sq. (Q2) Cut in half diagonally
  * Two - 4" x 14 3/4" (Q5)
- Five 2 1/2" x 42" strips for straight-grain binding.

▨ **From Fabric III, cut:  (bright red print)**
- Four 1 7/8" x 42" strips. From these, cut:
  * 128 - 1 1/8" x 1 7/8" (A2)

■ **From Fabric IV, cut:  (dark red print)**
- One 5" x 42" strip. From this, cut:
  * Thirty-two - 1" x 5" (A8)
  * Thirty-two - 1" squares (A9)
- One 4 1/2" x 42" strip. From this, cut:
  * Thirty-two - 1" x 4 1/2" (A7)

# Festive Crab Ring

## Ingredients
1 small package unflavored gelatin
1/4 cup water
2 - 8 oz. packages cream cheese
2 tablespoons cooking sherry
3/4 teaspoon seasoned salt
1 - 2 oz. jar chopped pimientos
1/8 teaspoon ground black pepper
1/4 cup snipped parsley
1 - 6 oz. package frozen king crab meat, thawed, drained and cut up. **I do not like imitation crab meat in this recipe. If I can't find it frozen I boil king crab legs!

## Instructions

Sprinkle gelatin over water to soften. Stir over hot water until dissolved. Beat into cream cheese until smooth. Stir in remaining ingredients. Pour into a 3 cup ring mold. Refrigerate at least 4 hours or until set. Turn out on a plate and serve with crackers.

- Six 1 1/8" x 42" strips. From these, cut:
  * 192 - 1 1/8" squares (A1a, A2a)

**From Fabric V, cut: (bright green print)**
- Two 1 7/8" x 42" strips. From these, cut:
  * Sixty-four - 1 1/8" x 1 7/8" (A5)
- Two 1 1/4" x 42" strips. From these, cut:
  * Sixty-four - 1 1/4" squares (A3)

**From Fabric VI, cut: (gold lamé)**
- One 1 3/4" x 42" strip. From this, cut:
  * Sixteen - 1 3/4" squares (A1) See Step 1 below.

## ASSEMBLY

### Poinsettia Block A Assembly

**1.** We had some scraps of gold lamé in the studio, and when I completed this design, I wanted something very classy looking for Christmas. Not too glittery, but just enough to glisten. We worked with the gold lamé and found it very flimsy to add the diagonal corners. Our solution was to press a fusible interfacing onto the back of the lamé. Use a press cloth. DO NOT place your iron on the lamé or it will melt. Cut the 1 3/4" squares from that.

**2.** For Block A, use diagonal corner technique to make eight of mirror image Unit 2, two of Unit 8a, and one of Unit 1.

**3.** To assemble the block, begin by joining mirror image Unit 2 in pairs as shown, matching seams. Make four pairs. Join two of the pairs to opposite ends of Unit 1 center.

**4.** For the corner triangles, join Unit 3 triangle to Unit 4 as shown; then add Unit 5 to the bottom. Trim off any points. Join Unit 6 to long diagonal side, being careful not to stretch the fabric because of the bias. Make four of the corners.

**5.** When assembling the corners, refer to block diagram frequently for correct placement as each one is turned when assembled. Join two corners to opposite sides of remaining Unit 2 pairs. Make two. Join these two sections to opposite sides of the center section.

**6.** Refer to instructions for making triangle-squares on page 7. Use this technique to make Unit 9 using 1" squares of fabrics I and IV. Join Unit 7 to opposite sides of Block A. Join triangle-square Unit 9 to one end of each Unit 8, referring to block diagram for correct positioning. Join this unit to opposite sides of Block A to complete it. Make 16.

### Table Runner Assembly

**1.** Refer to the diagram at right and join the 4 1/2" x 8 1/2" strips of fabrics I and II together. Cut them diagonally, and discard the areas shown.

**2.** Join four of Block A together as shown on the complete table runner diagram at right and turn them "on point." Make two of these combinations. Join the Q3 triangles to opposite sides to the 4-block combination matching the seams at the block corners.

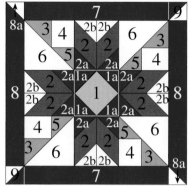

Block A. Make 16.
Finished size: 5 1/2" sq.

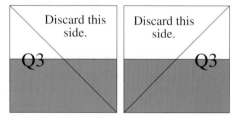

Make 4 each of mirror image Unit Q3

Press, and trim points. Handle the bias edges carefully so as not to stretch them. Join the Q3 triangles to remaining opposite sides. Press. This entire section should measure 14 5/8" square. Trim if necessary.

**3.** Join Unit Q4 to opposite sides of one Block A that is turned "on point." Press and trim points. Join Unit Q4 to remaining sides of the block. This section should measure 7 5/8" square. Make two and join them together, matching the Block A points. Join Unit Q5 to top and bottom of the two block section as shown.

**4.** For the ends of the table runner, join one short side of Unit Q1 triangle to Block A as shown. Join two of Block A together; then add them to the Q1-Block A combination. Add Unit Q2 triangles to each end of the combined blocks to complete the end sections.

**5.** Join the four Block A combination to opposite ends of the center section matching the seams of the large stripe. Don't be afraid to pin generously. Join the pointed tips to opposite ends of the table runner to complete the top.

### Finishing

**1.** Faye did some beautiful quilting on this piece to carry through with the subtle golden glisten. She quilted leaves on the outer green with gold metallic thread and "ditched" all of the patchwork with white thread.

**2.** Make approximately 180" of straight-grain binding from Fabric II, and bind the table runner.

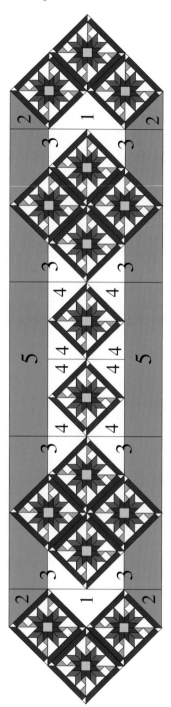

# Goose Tracks

**GOOSE TRACKS TABLE RUNNER**
Finishes to: 15 3/4" x 58 1/2".  Quick pieced.

## MATERIALS

| | | | |
|---|---|---|---|
| ■ | Fabric I  (medium olive print) | Need 12 1/8" | 3/8 yard |
| ■ | Fabric II  (dark rusty red print) | Need 9 1/4" | 3/8 yard |
| ■ | Fabric III  (yellow/gold check) | Need 14 1/2" | 1/2 yard |
| ■ | Fabric IV  (bright gold) | Need 7 1/2" | 1/4 yard |
| ■ | Fabric V  (medium blue print) | Need 5 1/8" | 1/4 yard |
| ■ | Fabric VI  (navy print) | Need 21 1/8" | 3/4 yard |
| ■ | Fabric VII  (dark brown print) | Need 3 3/8" | 1/8 yard |
| | Backing | 1  yard if backing is pieced. | |

## CUTTING

All "Q" units in cutting instructions stand for table runner top. These are units that are not incorporated into the specific blocks, but are on the table runner top.

Cutting instructions shown in red indicate that the quantity of units are combined and cut in two or more different places to conserve fabric.

**From Fabric I, cut:  (medium olive print)**
- One 6" x 42" strip.  From this, cut:
    * Two - 6" x 8 1/2" (B5, C5)
    * Two - 2 1/2" x 9 3/4" (B8, C8) stack this cut
    * Two - 3 5/8" squares (B18b, C18b)
    * Two - 1" x 2 7/8" (B31b, C31b)  stack this cut
    * Two - 1" x 2 1/2" (B3, C3)  stack this cut
    * Two - 1 3/4" x 2 3/8" (B18a, C18a)
- Two 2" x 42" strips.  From these, cut:

    * Twenty-four - 2" x 3 1/2" (A2)
- One 1 1/8" x 42" strip.  From this, cut:
    * Two - 1 1/8" x 2 1/4" (B17, C17)
    * Two - 1 1/8" squares (B15a, C15a)
    * Two - 1" x 4 5/8" (B10, C10)
    * Two - 1" x 2 1/8" (B19, C19)
    * Two - 1" x 2" (B21a, C21a)
- One 1" x 42" strip.  From this, cut:
    * One - 1" x 9" (Q2)
    * Eight - 1" squares (B4a, C4a, B13a, C13a, B24, C24, B31c, C31c)

**From Fabric II, cut:  (dark rusty red print)**
- One 3" x 42" strip.  From this, cut:
    * Eight - 3" squares (A1)  Cut in half diagonally

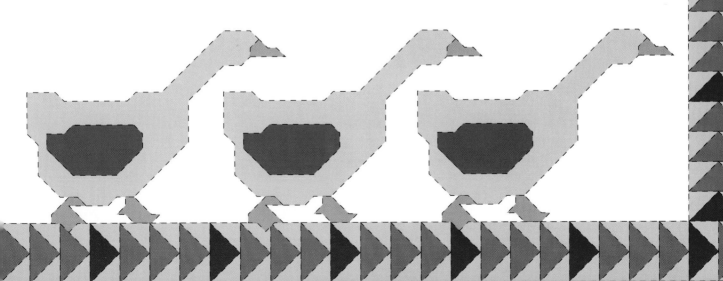

## Peach and Blueberry Cobbler

### Ingredients
12 - 15 ripe peaches, peeled
1 1/2 cups sugar
1 teaspoon cinnamon
1/3 cup packed brown sugar

1 - 12 oz. package of fresh blueberries
1 cup flour
1/2 teaspoon nutmeg
1 stick of butter

### Instructions
Rinse the blueberries in a colander, letting them drain well. Add blueberries to peaches and sprinkle with a tablespoon of sugar. Stir the sugar into the peaches and blueberries and let them sit for about 1/2 hour. Mix the dry ingredients together in a bowl. With a pastry blender, cut the butter into the dry ingredients until it is well blended. Divide in halves, and press one half into a well greased 9" x 12" x 2" pan. Sprinkle 1 tablespoon of flour over the peaches, and stir well into the peach/blueberry combination. Pour peach mixture over the bottom crust in the pan; then put the other half of the dry mixture on top, spreading it evenly. Bake at 350 for 30-35 minutes or until top is brown and bubbly.

Hi! My Name Is Katie! I live here and swim in the pond.

* Two - 1 1/2" x 2 1/2" (B1, C1) stack this cut
* Two - 1 1/2" squares (B28a, C28a) stack this cut
* Six - 1" x 1 1/2" (B26, C26, B29a, C29a) stack this cut
* Two - 1" x 2 1/2" (B23, C23)
* Four - 1" x 2" (Q1, B21a, C21a)
• Two 2" x 42" strips. From these, cut:
* Two - 2" x 9 3/4" (B7, C7)
* Two - 2" x 6" (B6, C6)
* Eight - 2" x 3 1/2" (A3)
* Two - 2" x 2 1/2" (B4b, C4b)
* Two - 2" x 2 1/4" (B27, C27)
* Two - 2" x 2 1/8" (B20, C20)
* Two - 1 7/8" x 2" (B30, C30)
• Two 1 1/8" x 42" strip. From this, cut:
* Two - 1 1/8" x 30 1/2" (Q3)
* Ten - 1" squares (B2a, C2a, B22a, C22a, B25, C25, B28b, C28b)

### From Fabric III, cut: (yellow/gold check)
• One 6 1/2" x 42" strip. From this, cut:
* Two - 3 1/8" x 6 1/2" (B9, C9)
* Two - 1 3/4" x 6 1/2" (B18, C18)
* Two - 1 7/8" x 5" (B11, C11)
* Two - 2 1/2" x 4" (B4, C4)
* Two - 2 5/8" x 2 7/8" (B13, C13) stack this cut
* Two - 2 1/2" squares (B5a, C5a) stack this cut
* Two - 1 1/2" x 2" (B14a, C14a) stack this cut
* Two - 1 1/2" squares (B1a, C1a) stack this cut
* Two - 1 1/8" x 1 5/8" (B15, C15) stack this cut
* Two - 1" x 2 3/4" (B31, C31) stack this cut
* Two - 1" x 2 1/4" (B16, C16) stack this cut
* Two - 1" x 1 3/8" (B10a, C10a) stack this cut
* Six - 1" squares (B12a, C12a) stack this cut
• Four 2" x 42" strips. From these, cut:
* Sixty-eight - 2" squares (A2a, A3a, B8a, C8a, B12b, C12b)

### From Fabric IV, cut: (bright gold print)
• One 3 1/2" x 42" strip. From this, cut:
* Two - 3 1/2" squares (A4)
* Two - 1 1/2" x 2 1/2" (B29, C29) stack this cut
* Two - 1 1/2" x 2" (B21, C21) stack this cut
* Two - 1 1/2" squares (B1a, C1a) stack this cut
* Two - 1" x 2 1/2" (B28, C28) stack this cut
* Two - 1" x 14 1/4" (Q5) stack this cut
* Four - 1" x 2 1/2" (B2, C2, B22, C22) stack this cut
* Two - 1" x 2" (B31a, C31a) stack this cut
* Two - 1" squares (B25, C25) stack this cut
• Four 1" x 42" strips. From these, cut:
* Four - 1" x 28 1/4" (Q4) Join two together to = 56"

### From Fabric V, cut: (medium blue print)
• One 5 1/8" x 42" strip. From this, cut:
* Four - 5 1/8" squares (A5) Cut in half diagonally.

### From Fabric VI, cut: (navy print)
• One 5 1/8" x 42" strip. From this, cut:
* Four - 5 1/8" squares (A6) Cut in half diagonally
* Two - 1 1/2" x 16 1/4" (Q7) stack this cut
• Four 2 1/2" x 42" strips for straight-grain binding
• Four 1 1/2" x 42" strips. From these, cut:
* Four - 1 1/2" x 28 3/4" (Q6) Join 2 together to = 57"

### From Fabric VII, cut: (dark brown print)
• One 3 3/8" x 42" strip. From this, cut:

* Two - 3 3/8" x 5" (B12, C12)
* Two - 1 1/2" x 2 7/8" (B14, C14)

## ASSEMBLY

### Flying Geese Block A
**1.** Use diagonal corner technique to make twelve of Unit 2, and four of Unit 3.
**2.** To piece the block, join three of Unit 2 in a row. Make 4 rows. Refer to diagram and join Unit 1 triangles to pointed ends of the combined "geese", Unit 2's. Join Unit 3 to the unpointed ends of each row. For center section, join the flying geese rows to opposite sides of center Unit 4.
**3.** For the sides, join triangle units 5 and 6 as shown. Make 4. Join the 5-6 combined units to opposite long sides of the two remaining "geese" rows. Join these rows to opposite sides of center section to complete the block. Make two and set aside.

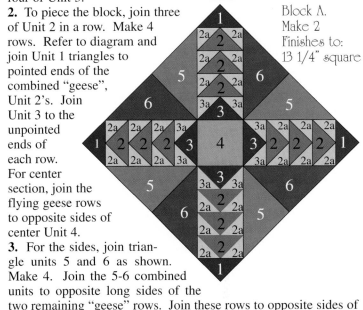

Block A.
Make 2
Finishes to:
13 1/4" square

### Goose Blocks B and C
**1.** Use diagonal corner technique to make two each of mirror image units 1, 2, 4, 5, 8, 12, 13, 15, 18b, 22, and 28.
**2.** To make mirror image Unit 1,

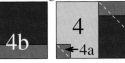

Use this assembly for Blocks B & C, Unit 1, and 25.
For Unit 1, place 1 1/2" squares of fabric III, and IV together, matching raw edges, and stitch a diagonal line down the center as shown. Press open and trim center seam, leaving the top and base fabric.
For Unit 25, place 1" squares of fabrics II and IV right sides together, and stitch as directed for Unit 1.

and Unit 25, refer to drawings and instructions in gold box above. After the triangle-squares are complete, refer to the diagram below for making Unit 1. The triangle-squares are now used as diagonal corners. Stitch the diagonals as shown or mirror images. Trim seam and press.
**3.** To make Unit 4, join the 1" x 2 1/2" piece of Fabric I with the 2" x 2 1/2" piece of Fabric II, forming a square.

Making Unit 1

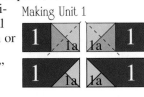

This square is now used as a diagonal corner. Refer to illustration of Unit 4 and with right sides together, place the mirror image 4b squares as shown and stitch the diagonal. Trim seam and press; then add diagonal corner 4a.

Making Unit 4

**4.** Use diagonal end technique to make two each of mirror image units 10, 14, 18, 21, 29, and 31. Refer to diagrams on page 76 showing how the units are assembled.

**5.** For Unit 21, join 1" x 2" pieces of fabrics I and IV. making a small strip. This strip is now used as a diagonal corner. Refer to the illustration below for correct placement of mirror image units. Unit 31 is a continuous diagonal end, with one diagonal corner which is added last. Refer to page 7 and the diagram below for making continuous diagonal corners.

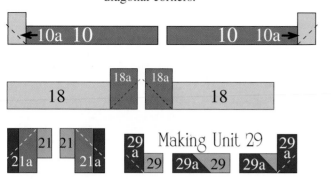

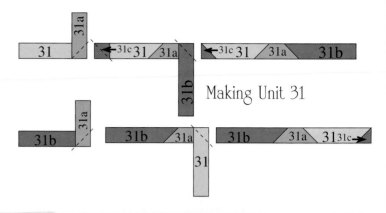

Making Unit 31

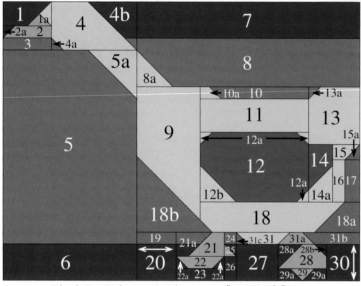

Making Unit 29

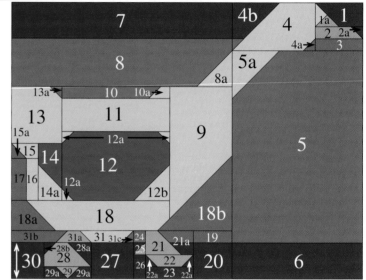

Block B. Make 1. Finishes to: 12" x 15 1/4"

Block C. Make 1. Finishes to: 12" x 15 1/4"

**6.** To assemble the block, refer frequently to the diagrams above for correct placement of mirror image units. Begin by joining units 1, 2, and 3 in a row; then add Unit 4 as shown. Join units 5 and 6. Join these combined units to goose head combined units and set aside.

**7.** Join units 7 and 8. Join units 10, 11, and 12 in a vertical row. Join units 16 and 17; then add Unit 15 to top of these combined units, matching seams. Join Unit 14 to side; then join Unit 13 to top. Join the combined 13-17 units to the 10-12 combined units, matching the wing seam. Join Unit 18 to bottom; then add Unit 9 as shown. Join diagonal corner 18b as shown. Add the combined 7-8 units to top of goose body.

**8.** For the feet section, begin by joining units 19 and 20. Join units 21, 22, and 23 in a vertical row and join them to the combined 19-20 units. Join units 24, 25, and 26 in a row. Add these to the 19-23 combined units. Join units 28 and 29, Refer to diagram for correct placement of the mirror image units and add Unit 27 to one side of combined 28-29 units, and Unit 30 to the other side. Join Unit 31 to top of these combined units, matching leg seam. Join the two combined unit sections together to complete the feet.

**9.** Join the feet to the body, matching the front foot and body seams. Join the two completed goose sections together matching the neck seam to complete blocks B and C.

**10.** To assemble the table runner, refer to the illustration at the top of page 77. Begin by joining units Q1, Q2, and Q1 together. Join

geese blocks B and C to opposite sides of this small center section. Join Unit Q3 to top and bottom of the geese. Join Block A to opposite sides of the geese. Join border Q4 to top and bottom of table runner; then join Unit Q5 to opposite short sides. Join border Unit Q6 to top and bottom of table runner; then add Unit Q7 to opposite sides to complete the top.

**Finishing**
**1.** Faye quilted some charming little flowers with leaves in the large open green sections. The patchwork was "ditched."
2. Join the four 2 1/2" strips of Fabric VI and make approximately 160" of straight-grain binding and bind the table runner.

GOOSE TRACKS PLACE MAT
Finishes to: 14" x 18 1/4"

## MATERIALS FOR FOUR PLACE MATS

Fabric I (medium olive print)    Need 12"
1/2 yard

Fabric II (dark rusty red print)   Need 9 1/2"
3/8 yard

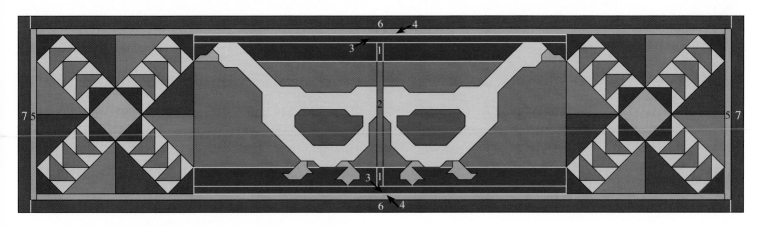

## Block A

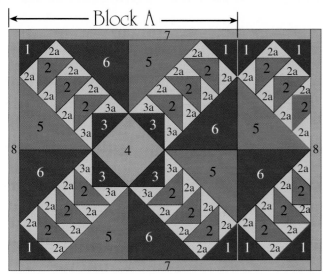

| | |
|---|---|
| Fabric III (yellow/gold check) | Need 18" |
| 5/8 yard | |
| Fabric IV (bright gold) | Need 28 7/8" |
| 1 yard | |
| Fabric V (medium blue print) | Need 10 1/4" |
| 3/8 yard | |
| Fabric VI (navy print) | Need 10 1/4" |
| 3/8 yard | |
| Backing We used 16" x 20 1/2" | |
| 1 yard | |

## CUTTING FOR FOUR PLACE MATS

**From Fabric I, cut: (medium olive print)**
• Six 2" x 42" strips. From these, cut:
  * Seventy-two - 2" x 3 1/2" (A2)

**From Fabric II, cut: (dark rusty/red print)**
• One 3 1/2" x 42" strip. From this, cut:
  * Sixteen - 2" x 3 1/2" (A3)
• Two 3" x 42" strips. From these, cut:
  * Sixteen - 3" squares (A1) Cut in half diagonally

**From Fabric III, cut: (yellow/gold check)**
• Nine 2" x 42" strips. From these, cut:
  * 184 - 2" squares (A2a, A3a)

**From Fabric IV, cut: (bright gold)**
• One 3 1/2" x 42" strip. From this, cut:
  * Four - 3 1/2" squares (A4)
  * Three - 1 1/8" x 17 1/2" (Q7) stack this cut

• Seven 2 1/2" x 42" strips for straight-grain binding
• Seven 1 1/8" x 42" strips. From these, cut:
  * Five - 1 1/8" x 17 1/2" (add to Q7)
  * Eight - 1 1/8" x 14 1/2" (Q8)

**From Fabric V, cut: (medium blue print)**
• Two 5 1/8" x 42" strips. From these, cut:
  * Ten - 5 1/8" squares (A5) Cut in half diagonally

**From Fabric VI, cut: (navy print)**
• Two 5 1/8" x 42" strips. From these, cut:
  * Ten - 5 1/8" squares (A6) Cut in half diagonally

## ASSEMBLY

**1.** Follow instructions for the table runner, Block A on page 75. To complete one place mat you will need to make two more sets (per place mat) of the Unit 2 geese blocks. Refer to the diagram of the place mat and join Unit 1 to the pointed ends of the Unit 2 combined "geese." Join another Unit 1 triangle to the opposite side of the tip triangle as shown in diagram. Place so that the triangles overlap 1/4" when sewn for your seam allowance.

**2.** Join triangle Unit 5 to side of one "geese" combination, and Unit 6 triangle to the other. Using the large triangles as a guide, join the two "geese" sections together.

**3.** Trim along the side as shown, using triangles, Unit 1 as a guide. Line your ruler up with the raw edges of the Unit 1 triangles and trim off the excess of two of the Unit 2's.

**4.** Join this section to Block A, matching seams. Join Unit Q7 to top and bottom of place mat; then add Unit 8 to opposite sides to complete the place mat top.

**Finishing**

**1.** Quilt the place mats "in the ditch." Join the seven 2 1/2" strips of Fabric IV for the binding, and bind your place mat set.

# Peppermint Ice Cream

## Peppermint Ice Cream Pie

### Ingredients

20 Oreo cookies
1/4 stick of butter, melted
1 1/2 quarts vanilla ice cream
1 teaspoon peppermint flavoring
8 peppermint candies, crushed
12 drops red food coloring

### Instructions

Crush the Oreo cookies in a food processor and add the melted butter. Press into a 9-inch pie plate. Soften the ice cream, either in the microwave or allow it to defrost at room temperature until it is soft enough to fold in the candies, flavoring and coloring. Mix well. Pour the ice cream mixture onto the crust and freeze.

### Hot Fudge Sauce Ingredients

1 stick of butter
4 squares of unsweetened chocolate
3 cups of sugar
1/2 teaspoon salt
1 large can evaporated milk

### Instructions For Hot Fudge Sauce

Melt the butter in the top of a double boiler. Drop in the chocolate and stir until melted. Add sugar a little at a time, stirring well until it is all added. Add salt. Slowly stir in evaporated milk. After all of the milk has been added, let the mixture cook over the hot water until all of the sugar is completely dissolved. Stir occasionally.
This sauce keeps in the refrigerator for a long time. Always warm sauce before it is served. Heat and pour over the pie slices when they are served.

## PEPPERMINT ICE CREAM TABLECLOTH
Finishes to 54" square. Quick pieced.

## MATERIALS

| | | |
|---|---|---|
| ☐ | Fabric I (white on white print) | Need 25" |
| | 7/8 yard | |
| ■ | Fabric II (burgundy print) | Need 45" |
| | 1 3/8 yards | |
| ◼ | Fabric III (medium rose batik) | Need 39" |
| | 1 1/4 yards | |
| ◻ | Fabric IV (medium pink print) | Need 37 1/2" |
| | 1 1/8 yards | |
| ◻ | Fabric V (pale mint green print) | Need 27 1/2" |
| | 7/8 yard | |
| ◼ | Fabric VI (medium mint green print) | Need 31 1/2" |
| | 1 yard | |

## CUTTING

Cutting instructions shown in red indicate that the quantity of units are combined and cut in two or more different places to conserve fabric.

**From Fabric I, cut: (white on white print)**
- Four 5 3/8" x 42 1/2" strips. From this, cut:
  * Two - 5 3/8" x 42 1/2" (15)
  * Two - 5 3/8" x 32 3/4" (14)
  * Four - 3 3/4" squares (basket squares)
- One 3 3/4" wide strip. From this, cut:
  * Eight - 3 3/4" squares (add to 3 3/4" sq. above)
- Three 3 1/2" x 42" strips for Strip Set 1

**From Fabric II, cut: (burgundy print)**
- Two 7 5/8" x 42 1/4" strips. From these, cut:
  * Four - 7 5/8" x 13 3/8" (basket handle)
  * Four - 5" x 7 1/4" (7)
  * Four - 3 1/2" squares (13)
- One 2 3/4" x 42" strip. From this, cut:
  * Eight - 2 3/4" squares (6a)
- Six 2 1/2" wide strips for straight-grain binding.
- Six 2" x 42" strip. From these, cut:
  * Fifty-six - 2" x 3 1/2" (2)
  * Twenty - 2" squares (4, 15a)

**From Fabric III, cut: (medium rose batik)**
- One 11" x 42" strip. From this, cut:
  * Two - 11" squares (cut in half diagonally for basket lining)
  * Two - 4 1/4" squares (2a)
  * Six - 4 1/8" squares (basket triangles) cut in half diagonally.
- Two 4 1/4" x 42" strips. From these, cut:
  * Twelve - 4 1/4" squares (add to 4 1/4" squares above)
  * Seven - 3 3/4" squares (basket squares)
- Two 3 3/4" x 42" strips. From these, cut:
  * Five - 3 3/4" squares (add to basket squares above)
  * Eight - 2" x 3 1/2" (3)
- Six 2" x 42" strips for Strip Set 1.

**From Fabric IV, cut: (medium pink print)**
- Two 12 1/2" x 42" strips. From these, cut:
  * Four - 12 1/2" squares (napkins)
  * Four - 2" x 3 1/2" (15a corner)
  * Eighty-eight - 2" squares (1a, 3a, 15a corners)
- Two 4 1/4" x 42" strips. From these, cut:
  * Fourteen - 4 1/4" squares (2a)
  * Twenty - 2" squares (add to 2" squares above)
- Two 2" x 42" strips. From these, cut:
  * Forty - 2" squares (add to 2" squares above)

**From Fabric V, cut: (pale mint green print)**
- One 14 1/2" x 42" strip. From this, cut:
  * One - 14" square (5)
  * Four - 7 1/4" squares (8) stack this cut
  * Four - 5" x 7 1/4" (6) stack this cut
- One 5" x 42" strip. From this, cut:
  * Four - 5" x 7 1/4" (add to 6 above)
- Four 2" x 42" strips. From these, cut:
  * Two - 2" x 30 1/2" (10)
  * Two - 2" x 27 1/2" (9)

**From Fabric VI, cut: (medium mint green print)**
- Two 12 1/2" x 42" strips. From these, cut:
  * Four - 12 1/2" squares (napkins)
- Four 1 5/8" x 42" strips. From these, cut:
  * Two - 1 5/8" x 32 3/4" (12)
  * Two - 1 5/8" x 30 1/2" (11)

## ASSEMBLY

**Making The Strip Set**

**1.** Refer to page 6 for strip piecing techniques. The illustration at right shows the strip set to be made. Follow the instructions and cut the thirty-two 3 1/2" segments. Use diagonal corner technique to make thirty-two of Strip Set, Unit 1. The completed unit should measure 3 1/2" x 6 1/2"

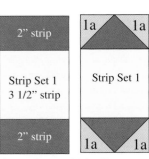

Strip Set 1. Make 3.
Cut into thirty-two 3 1/2" segments. Join diagonal corners after strip set has been cut.

80

## Quarter square triangles, Unit 2a. Make 14 to yield 28, using 4 1/4" sq. of fabrics III & IV.

   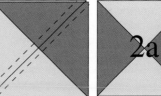  

Wrong side of lightest fabric. Solid line is cutting line. Dashed lines are stitch lines. Stitch on dashed lines and cut on solid line. This will yield two triangle-squares.

This diagram shows correct placement.

Center line is cut line, and dashed lines are seam lines. With right sides together, and raw edges matching, place the triangle-squares together as shown above. This will yield two quarter triangles for Unit 2a.

### Making the Quarter Square Triangles.

1. Refer to page 9 for making triangle-squares with The Angler 2. The quarter square triangles shown above are made using this method. If you are not using The Angler 2, draw a diagonal line from corner to corner on the back of the lightest fabric as shown. Place the 4 1/4" squares of fabrics III and IV right sides together. Stitch 1/4" on both sides of the drawn center line. Cut on the solid drawn line. This yields two triangle-squares. Press open and trim tips. Join Unit 2 to top and bottom of quarter square triangles as shown in large drawing of tablecloth.

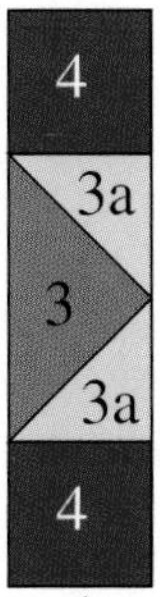

2. Once again refer to illustration above and place two of the triangle-squares right sides together as shown in center drawing. Draw diagonal line as shown on the back of one of the squares. Place squares right sides together as shown, and stitch 1/4" on both sides of the center. Cut the squares apart on the drawn center line. Trim tips and press open. This is now Unit 2a which should measure 3 1/2" square. Join Unit 2 to opposite ends of Unit 2a as shown in large drawing of the tablecloth. Refer to the drawing for correct position of Unit 2a. The completed unit will measure 3 1/2" x 6 1/2".

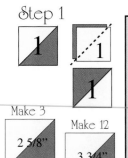

Make 8

### Step 1

Make 3

Make 12

2 5/8"

For Place Mat

3 3/4"

For Basket

Use this assembly for basket triangle-squares on tablecloth and place mat.
1. For tablecloth, place 3 3/4" squares of fabrics I and III right sides together, matching raw edges, and stitch a diagonal line down the center as shown. Press open and trim center seam, leaving the top and base fabric.
2. For place mat, place 2 5/8" squares of fabrics I and III right sides together. Stitch as instructed above.

3. The combined Unit 3-4 above left is used in the corners of the tablecloth. Use diagonal corner technique to make eight of Unit 3.
4. Join Unit 4 to opposite short ends of Unit 3. This combined unit should measure 2" x 6 1/2". Set aside.

### Making The Basket

1. Refer to instructions in gold box above, and the diagrams next to it. The 3 3/4" squares are for the basket (1). Refer to the drawing at right for placement of the squares. To assemble the basket, begin in top right corner and join two of square 1 and one triangle. Follow the diagram, joining one square 1 with another triangle. Join these two rows together; then add final triangle to left side.

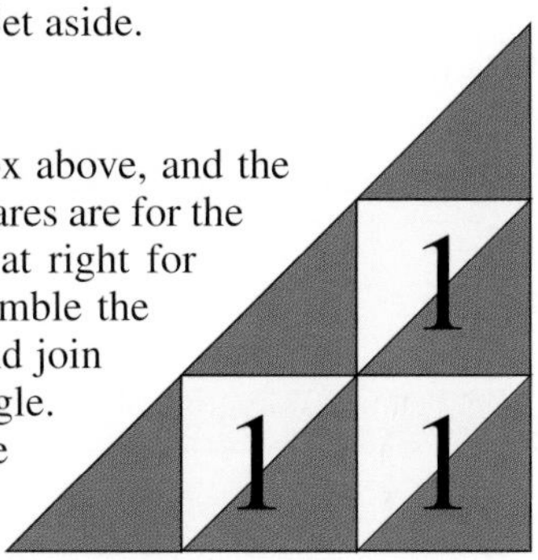

Use 11" square of fabric III, cut in half diagonally for lining.

2. Cut the 11" square of Fabric III in half diagonally and use it as a basket lining. Place the pieced basket on top of the larger triangle, and trim the lining triangle to match the basket top if necessary. With right sides together, stitch around the basket, leaving an opening to turn. Turn right side out, and use a small strip of Steam-A-Seam 2 to close the opening. Handle the triangles carefully so as not to distort them as the bias can stretch easily. Set baskets aside.

3. The basket handle is on the large pattern sheet. Cut it out as directed on the pattern sheet. Refer to page 11 for appliqué instructions. Prepare the basket handles for appliqué and set aside.

### Preparing The Corners

1. Refer to illustration of Unit 15 below. As Unit 15 is 5 3/8" x 42 1/2", we are showing only a portion of it so that the diagonal corner may be prepared. There are two units from Fabric IV for this corner. The long one shown below measures 2" x 3 1/2, and the other is a 2" square. The remaining 15a unit is from Fabric II, and it also measures 2" square. To make the corner, join the 2" - 15a squares together as shown; then add the 2" x 3 1/2" 15a unit to the side. This pieced square will measure 3 1/2" and will now become a diagonal corner.

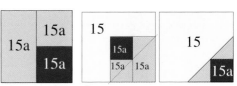

15a corner. Make 4.

Refer to illustration of complete tablecloth on page 82 for correct placement of this diagonal corner on Unit 15. The illustration above shows how to place the diagonal corner on Unit 15. With right sides together, and raw edges matching, place the diagonal corner square as shown, and stitch the diagonal. Trim center seam and press. Complete all four corners.

### Tablecloth Assembly.

1. Using the 14" square of Fabric V, place the basket handles as shown in the illustration. The straight short ends of the handles will be pressed in place so that they line up with the raw edges of the 14" square. Lay all four basket handles out on top of the 14" square as shown. When you are satisfied with their placement, press them in place. Place a stabilizer behind the square. We used a blanket stitch around the handles with burgundy rayon thread. Tear away the stabilizer when the handles are completed.
2. Use diagonal corner technique to make eight of mirror image Unit 6. Refer to the large drawing for correct placement of diagonal corner 6a. When assembling the top, please note that Unit 7 is shown on the tablecloth diagram. The baskets will be stitched on top of it. Unit 7 completes the base for the baskets.
3. To assemble the center of the tablecloth, begin by joining Unit 8, Unit 6, Unit 7, Unit 6 and Unit 8 in a row. Make 2. Check the diagram for correct placement of mirror image Unit 6. For center section of the tablecloth, join Unit 6, Unit 7 and mirror image Unit

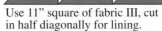

6 together as shown.  Make two.  Join the two combined 6-7-6 units to opposite ends of center square Unit 5, catching the short ends of the basket handles into the seams.

**4.** Join the combined units made in Step 3 to opposite long sides of the center section and press seams towards the center.  Join Unit 9 to opposite sides of center section; then add Unit 10 to opposite sides as shown.  Join border Unit 11 to opposite sides of center; then add border Unit 12.  Complete the center by adding diagonal corner, Unit 13 as shown.  Place the basket pockets as shown on the diagram below.  Pin or baste them in place.  Top stitch the baskets in place along the edges, leaving the top long edge open for the napkin to fit into the pocket.

**5.** Join Unit 14 to opposite sides of center section; then add Unit 15, referring to diagram below for correct placement of corners.

**6.** The side borders will be completed first.  Refer frequently to the diagram below for correct placement.  Begin by joining seven of the completed Strip Set 1 units with quarter triangle square Unit 2, alternating them as shown.  Join combined units 3-4 to opposite ends of the pieced border, checking diagram for correct placement

of the 3-4 unit.  Make 2 of these borders.

**7.** For top and bottom borders, join nine of the Strip Set 1 units with quarter triangle square Unit 2, alternating them as shown.  Again, join combined units 3-4 to opposite ends of the border as shown.  Make two of this border and join to top and bottom of tablecloth top.  Be careful to match seams, and don't be afraid to PIN!!!

**Finishing**

**1.** Faye quilted lovely heart shaped feathery designs in the large open center sections, and carried the feather motif through on the large white section.  Small flowers were quilted in each white square of the border.

**2.** Make approximately 230" of straight-grain french fold binding from 2 1/2" wide strips of Fabric II, and bind your tablecloth.  Refer to page 11 for making our reversible napkins.  Make four napkins.  Refer to following page for the napkin fold.

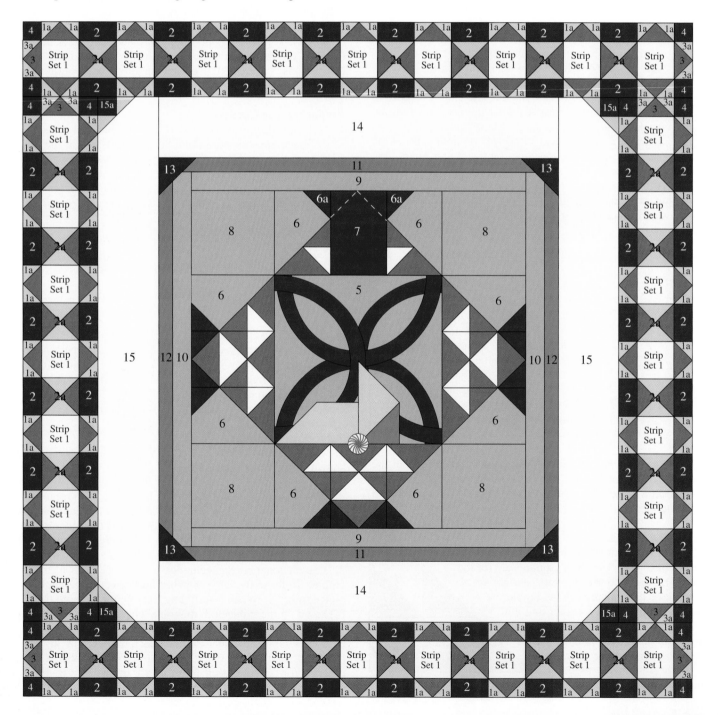

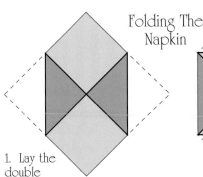
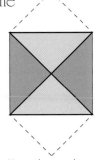

## Folding The Napkin

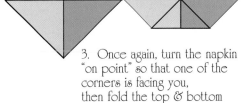

1. Lay the double sided napkin "on point." Fold the left & right corners to the center.

2. Turn the napkin over and fold the top & bottom corners to the center.

3. Once again, turn the napkin "on point" so that one of the corners is facing you, then fold the top & bottom corners to the center

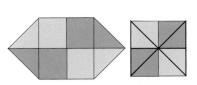
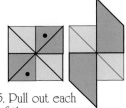
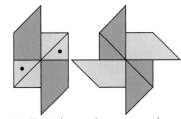

4. Turn the napkin over and fold the side corners to the center

5. Pull out each of the corners marked with a dot..

6. Turn the napkin over, and once again and pull out the corners marked with a dot. We used a peppermint candy to hold down the folds.

## MATERIALS FOR TWO PLACE MATS

| | | |
|---|---|---|
| ☐ | Fabric I (white on white print) 1/8 yard | Need 2 5/8" |
| ⬛ | Fabric II (burgundy print) 3/4 yard | Need 22 1/8" |
| ⬛ | Fabric III (medium rose batik) 1/4 yard | Need 7 1/2" |
| ⬜ | Fabric IV (medium pink print) 1/2 yard | Need 15" |
| ⬜ | Fabric V (pale mint green print) 1/2 yard | Need 12" |
| ⬜ | Fabric VI (med.. mint green print) 1 yard | Need 31 1/2" |

## CUTTING

☐ **From Fabric I, cut:  (white on white print)**
- One 2 5/8" x 42" strip. From this, cut:
  * Six - 2 5/8" squares (basket)
  * Twelve - 1 1/2" x 2 1/2" (6)
  * Four - 1 1/2" squares (2a, 8)

⬛ **From Fabric II, cut:  (burgundy print)**
- One 5 5/8" x 42" strip. From this, cut:
  * Two - 5 5/8" x 8 7/8" (basket handles)
  * Four - 3 1/2" squares (1a, 2a)
  * Eight - 2 1/2" squares (4)  stack this cut
- Four 3 1/2" x 42" strips for straight-grain binding.
- One 2 1/2" x 42" strip. From this, cut:
  * Six - 2 1/2" squares (add to 4)
  * Four - 2 1/4" x 2 1/2" (10)

⬛ **From Fabric III, cut:  (medium rose batik)**
- One 7 1/2" x 42" strip. From this, cut:
  * One - 7 1/2" square (cut in half diagonally for basket lining)

  * Three - 3" squares (cut in half diagonally for basket) stack this cut
  * Six - 2 5/8" squares (for basket)  stack this cut
  * Twelve - 2 1/2" squares (7) stack this cut
  * Two - 1 1/2" x 2 1/2" (2a) stack this cut
  * Thirty - 1 1/2" squares (2a, 5a, 9a) stack this cut

⬜ **From Fabric IV, cut:  (medium pink print)**
- One 12 1/2" x 42" strip. From this, cut:
  * Two - 12 1/2" squares (napkins)
  * Twenty-four - 2 1/2" squares (7a, 7b)  stack this cut
- One 2 1/2" x 42" strip. From this, cut:
  * Ten - 1 1/2" x 2 1/2" (5)
  * Eight - 1 1/2" x 2 1/4" (9)

⬜ **From Fabric V, cut:  (pale mint green print)**
- One 10 1/2" x 42" strip. From this, cut:
  * Two - 10" x 10 1/2" (2)
  * Two - 5 3/4" x 10 1/2" (1)
- One 1 1/2" x 42" strip. From this, cut:
  * Two - 1 1/4" x 15 1/2" (3)

⬜ **From Fabric VI, cut:  (medium mint green print)**
- One 12 1/2" x 42" strip. From this, cut:
  * Two - 12 1/2" squares (napkins)

Finishes to
14" X 18".
Quick
pieced.

## ASSEMBLY

**Instructions are for assembly of one place mat**
**Making The Place Mat**

1. Use diagonal corner technique to make six of Unit 7, five of Unit 5, four of Unit 9 and one each of units 1 and 2. Join the diagonal corners for Unit 7 in alphabetical order.

Place Mat Unit 2a

2. The top right corner for Unit 2 is shown at right. To make the corner, join the two 2 1/2" squares of fabrics I and III; then add the 1 1/2" x 2 1/2" piece of fabric III as shown. This square will now be used as a diagonal corner. Place the square, right sides together on Unit 2 as shown. Stitch the diagonal, trim the center seam, and press the square towards the corner.

3. To assemble the place mat, join units 1 and 2 together as shown, matching the diagonal corner seams. Add Unit 3 to bot-

Finishes to: 14" x 18"

tom.

To prepare the units for the borders, Join units 6 and 7. Make six. Join units 4 and 9. Make 3, referring to diagram above for correct placement of the units as they are mirror image. Join units 4 and 5. Make 5. Join units 8 and 9, making one. For the side border, join the combined 4-5 units with the combined 6-7 units, alternating them as shown. Join the combined 8-9 combined units to the top; then add the combined 4-9 units to the bottom, matching seams.

4. To assemble the top border, begin by joining combined units 6-7 and combined units 4-5, alternating them as shown. Join the combined 4-9 units to opposite ends to complete the top border. Join to the bottom of the place mat, matching seams.

5. For the basket, the handle is on the large pattern sheet. Refer to page 11 for appliqué instructions and trace the handle onto the Steam-A-Seam 2. Prepare the handle for applique. Refer to page 81 for the drawings and instructions in gold box to make the 2 5/8" triangle-squares for the basket. Read the instructions for Making The Basket and join the triangle-squares with the Fabric III triangles to complete the basket. Place the basket right sides down on the lining triangle, and trim the lining triangle if necessary. Stitch around the basket leaving an opening to turn. Turn right side out and close the opening with a small strip of Steam-A-Seam 2.

6. Pin the basket on the place mat. Place the handle so that the short ends extend down into the basket approximately 3/4". Place a piece of stabilizer behind the handle and run a blanket stitch around the handle. Top stitch the basket in place along the edge, leaving the top open for the napkin.

7. Refer to page 8 for making and applying the binding frame, and bind the place mat using the 3 1/2" wide strips of Fabric II. Refer to page 83 for making and folding the napkin.

# MOONLIGHT SERENADE

## Southwest Salsa

### Ingredients

8 Roma tomatoes
1 clove elephant garlic
2 jalapenos, diced
1 teaspoon fresh cilantro
1 teaspoon sugar

### Instructions

Combine ingredients and serve at room temperature.

## MOONLIGHT SERENADE TABLE RUNNER
### Finishes to: 53 1/2" square.
### Napkins finish to 13" square. Quick pieced.

## MATERIALS FOR TABLE RUNNER & 4 NAPKINS

Fabric I (dark purple dotted print) Need 61 1/4"
1 7/8 yards

Fabric II (light gold print) Need 10 3/8"
3/8 yard

Fabric III (med.. brown print) Need 9 7/8"
3/8 yard

Fabric IV (dark honey stripe) Need 3 1/2"
1/4 yard

Fabric V (medium rose print) Need 8"
3/8 yard

Fabric VI (dusty pink print) Need 35"
1 1/8 yards

Backing                          3 3/8 yards

## CUTTING FOR TABLE RUNNER & 4 NAPKINS

All "Q" units in cutting instructions stand for table runner top. These are units that are not incorporated into the specific blocks, but are on the table runner top.

Cutting instructions shown in red indicate that the quantity of units are combined and cut in two or more different places to conserve fabric.

### From Fabric I, cut: (dark purple dotted print)
• Six 2 1/2" x 42" strips. Five for straight-grain binding. From remaining strip, cut:
  * Four - 2 1/2" x 8 1/4" (A15)
• One 5 1/2" x 42" strip. From this, cut:
  * Five - 5 1/2" square (Q1)
  * Four - 2 1/2" x 5 1/2" (A13)
  * Four - 1 1/4" squares (A10a)
  * Four - 1 1/8" squares (A14a)
• One 4 3/8" x 42" strip. From this, cut:
  * Two - 4 3/8" squares (C4) Cut in half diagonally
  * Four - 3 7/8" squares (C3) Cut in half diagonally
  * Four - 1 5/8" squares (A7a)
  * Four - 1 1/4" x 2 3/8" (A11)
  * Four - 1 1/4" x 2" (A12)
• Three 3 1/2" x 42" strips. From these, cut:
  * Twenty-eight - 3 1/2" squares (A1a, Q4)
  * Eighteen - 1 1/2" x 3 1/4" (B2a, C2a, Q3a)
• Two 3 1/4" x 42" strips. From these, cut:
  * Forty-two - 1 1/2" x 3 1/4" (B2a, C2a, Q3a)
• One 2 7/8" x 42" strip. From this, cut:
  * Four - 2 7/8" squares (A5a)
  * Four - 2 5/8" x 7 1/2" (A9)
• Eleven 1 1/2" x 42" strips. From these, cut:
  * Eight - 1 1/2" x 14 1/4" (A16)
  * Twenty - 1 1/2" x 2 1/4" (Q2a)
  * 196- 1 1/2" squares (A7a, B1a, C1a)

### From Fabric II, cut: (light gold print)
• Two 3 7/8" x 42" strips. From these, cut:
  * Eight - 3 7/8" squares (A3a, A5a)
  * Four - 3 1/4" x 3 7/8" (A2)
  * Four - 3 3/4" x 9 1/2" (A1)
• One 2 5/8" x 42" strip. From this, cut:
  * Four - 2 5/8" x 5 3/8" (A9a)

### From Fabric III, cut: (medium honey print)
• Two 3 7/8" x 42" strips. From these, cut:
  * Four - 3 7/8" x 5 3/4" (A5)
  * Four - 3 7/8" x 4 5/8" (A3)
  * Four - 2 1/8" x 3 7/8" (A4)
  * Four - 1 7/8" x 3 1/2" (A7)
  * Four - 1 3/4" x 3 1/2" (A8)
  * Four - 1 5/8" squares (A6c) stack this cut
  * Four - 1 1/2" x 2 1/2" (A14) stack this cut
  * Four - 1 1/4" x 2 3/8" (A12a) stack this cut
  * Eight - 1 1/4" squares (A6b, A11a) stack this cut
• One 2 1/8" x 42" strip. From this, cut:
  * Eight - 2 1/8" squares (A2a, A6a)
  * Eight - 1 1/8" squares (A15a)

### From Fabric IV, cut: (dark honey diamond print)
• One 3 1/2" x 42" strip. From this, cut:
  * Four - 3 1/2" x 4 3/4" (A6)
  * Four - 1 1/4" x 5" (A10)
  * Eight - 1 1/4" squares (A11a, A11b)

### From Fabric V, cut: (medium rose print)
• Two 4" x 42" strips. From these, cut:
  * Forty-eight - 1 1/2" x 4" (Q2, Q3, B2, C2)

### From Fabric VI, cut: (dusty pink print)
• Two 13 1/2" x 42" strips. From these, cut:
  * Four - 13 1/2" squares for napkins.
• Two 4" x 42" strips. From these, cut:
  * Ninety-six - 1 1/2" x 4" (B1, C1)

## ASSEMBLY

### Making The Coyote Block A
1. Use diagonal corner technique to make one each of units 1, 2, 3, 5, 6, 7, 10, 11, 14, and 15. To make Unit 5, refer to the diagram below, and begin by using the diagonal corner technique to make Unit 5a. This unit will now be used as a diagonal corner. Place the 5a corner on Unit 5 as shown, right sides together. Stitch the diagonal, trim the center seam and press corner towards the right.

Making Unit 5 for Block A

2. Use diagonal end technique to make one each of units 9 and 12. Refer to the illustrations at right to assemble the units.

Making Unit A9

Making Unit A12

3. Refer to the Block A illustration. To assemble the coyote, begin by joining units 2 and 3 as shown. Join units 4 and 5. Join units 8, 7-and 6 in a horizontal row. Join the 2-3 combined units to the 4-5 combined units; then add the combined 8-7-6 units to the bottom of the other combined units matching the tail seam. Join Unit 9 to the left side of the combined units; then add Unit 1 to the top.

4. Join units 12, 11, and 10 in a horizontal row. Add this row to the bottom of the coyote. Join units 13, 14, and 15 in a vertical row as shown. Join this row to the left side of the coyote. Add Unit 16 to opposite sides of the coyote to complete the block. Make 4.

### Making Block B
1. Use diagonal corner technique to make four of

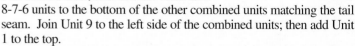

Making units 2 and 3 for Blocks B and C

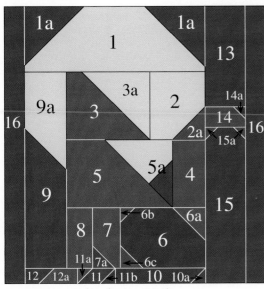

Block A. Make 4.
Finishes to: 13 1/2" x 14 1/4"

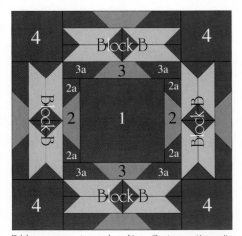

Block B. Make 4 for table runner.
Make 16 for napkins.
Finishes to: 3 1/2" x 7 1/2"

**Unit 1.** Refer to the diagram at the bottom of page 86, and use diagonal end technique to make one of Unit 2.

**2.** To assemble the block, refer to Block B diagram below and join four of Unit 1 as shown. Add Unit 2 to the top to complete Block B. Make 4.

Block C.
Make 4.

13 1/2" unfinished. Includes seam allowance.

## Making Point Block C

**1.** This block is made the same way as Block B. Follow Step 1 for Block B. Make two of Unit 2 as shown below.

**2.** Join the block as you did for Block B. Add another Unit 2 to the bottom. Join the side triangle Unit 3 to opposite sides; then join Unit 4 triangle to bottom. Line your ruler up along the triangular edges and trim as shown to complete Block C.

## Assembling The Center Section.

**1.** Refer to the diagram at right of the table runner center section. Use diagonal end technique to make two each of units Q2 and Q3.

**2.** Join Unit Q2 to opposite sides of Unit Q1; then join Unit Q3 to top and bottom of center section. Join Block B to opposite sides of the center section. Join Unit Q4 to opposite sides of the remaining Q4 units; then add them to top and bottom of the center section.

Table runner center and napkins. Center section units are all "Q" units. Finishes to 13 1/2" square. Make 1 for table runner. Make four for napkins.

## Table Runner Assembly.

**1.** To assemble the table runner, begin by joining Block C to Block A, joining the long side of the triangular Block C to the bottom of Block A. Refer to the diagram of the table runner, and join the combined A and C blocks to opposite sides of the center section. Press seams and join the remaining combined A and C blocks to the top and bottom of the table runner.

## Napkins

**1.** Refer to center section assembly and make four center sections which are used for the napkins.

**2.** Refer to page 11 for making reversible napkins. Use the pieced front and Fabric VI back.

# Reap What You Sew

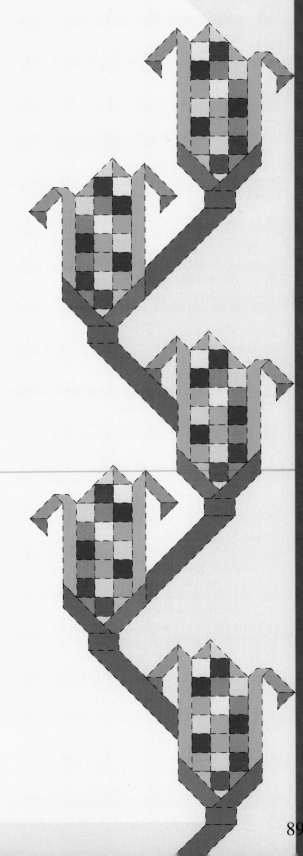

## Southwestern Style Corn Bread

*Ingredients*

1 3/4 cups cornmeal
1 tablespoon sugar
1 teaspoon baking powder
1 teaspoon baking soda
3/4 teaspoon salt
2 large eggs
2 cups buttermilk
1-2 fresh jalapeño peppers, seeded and minced
1/2 red pepper, seeded and minced
1 cup grated, sharp cheddar cheese
1 tablespoon vegetable shortening

*Instructions*

Whisk together thoroughly in a large bowl, the corn-meal, sugar, baking powder, baking soda and salt. Whisk the eggs until foamy in another bowl. Whisk in the buttermilk.
Add the wet ingredients to the dry ingredients along with the peppers and whisk just until blended.
Sprinkle the cheese over the batter and fold in. Preheat the oven to 400. Place the shortening in a heavy 9 inch cast iron skillet, and put in the hot oven until it smokes. Pour in the batter all at once and bake 20-25 minutes, or until the top is browned and the center feels firm when pressed.
Serve immediately from the pan. Cut into wedges with butter.

REAP WHAT YOU SEW TABLE RUNNER.
Finishes to: 22 3/8" X 67".
Quick pieced.

# MATERIALS

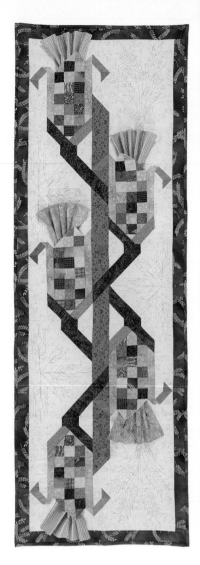

| | | | |
|---|---|---|---|
| ▢ | Fabric I (light yellow print) | Need 41 7/8" | 1 1/4 yards |
| ▢ | Fabric II (very dark olive print) | Need 9 1/4" | 3/8 yard |
| ▢ | Fabric III (dark olive print) | Need 5 3/4" | 1/4 yard |
| ▢ | Fabric IV (medium olive print) | Need 4 1/4" | 1/4 yard |
| ▢ | Fabric V (bright lime green) | Need 2 7/8" | 1/8 yard |
| ▢ | Fabric VI (light olive print) | Need 6" | 1/4 yard |
| ▢ | Fabric VII (bright yellow print) | Need 1 3/4" | 1/8 yard |
| ▢ | Fabric VIII (rust print) | Need 24 1/2" | 3/4 yard |
| ▢ | Fabric IX (bright gold print) | Need 25" | 7/8 yard |
| ▢ | Fabric X (gold stripe) | Need 25" | 7/8 yard |
| ▥ | Fabric X1 (assorted colors of red, orange, yellow, rust and brown) | | Scraps |
| | Backing | | 2 yards |

All "Q" units in cutting instructions stand for table runner top. These are units that are not incorporated into the specific blocks, but are on the table runner top.

Cutting instructions shown in red indicate that the quantity of units are combined and cut in two or more different places to conserve fabric.

# CUTTING

▢ **From Fabric I, cut: (light yellow print)**
- Two 9" x 42" strips. From these, cut:
  - Two - 9" x 14 3/4" (Q2)
  - One - 9" x 11 3/4" (Q11)
  - One - 9" x 9 5/8" (Q3)
  - One - 9" square (Q10)
  - Five - 2 7/8" x 7 5/8" (A14, B14)
  - Five - 2 1/2" squares (A8a, B8a Q3b, Q10b, Q11b) stack this cut
  - Seven - 1 3/4" squares (A12, B12, E3, F3) stack this cut
- From scrap, cut:
  - Five - 1 1/8" square (A6a, B6a)
- Two 4 3/4" x 42" strips. From these, cut:
  - Five 4 3/4" x 11 1/2" (corn lining)
  - Five - 1 3/4" x 4 3/4" (A15, B15)
  - One - 4 5/8" x 11 1/2" (A1, B1)
- Two 4 5/8" x 42" strips. From these, cut:
  - Four - 4 5/8" x 11 1/2" (add to A1, B1)
  - Two - 2 7/8" x 4 3/8" (E4a, F4a)
  - Two - 2 7/8" x 3 1/4" (E1, F1)
  - Five - 2 1/4" squares (A11a, B11a)
  - Two - 2" x 11 3/8" (Q1) stack this cut
  - Seven - 1 5/8" squares (A11b, B11b, E1b, F1b)
- One 2 5/8" x 42" strip. From this, cut:
  - Five - 2 5/8" x 2 7/8" (A10, B10)
  - Five - 1 1/2" x 2 5/8" (A5, B5)
  - Seven - 1 5/8" x 1 3/4" (A13, B13, E2, F2)
- One 2 1/2" x 42" strip. From this, cut
  - Five - 2 1/2" squares (add to 2 1/2" sq. above)

- Five - 1 3/4" x 2 1/2" (A17, B17)
- Five - 2 3/8" squares (A9a, B9a)
- Five - 1 1/2" x 1 7/8" (A7a, B7a)

▢ **From Fabric II, cut: (very dark olive print)**
- One 5 1/8" x 42" strip. From this, cut:
  - Three - 2 7/8" x 5 1/8" (Q8, C2, D2)
  - Five - 4 3/4" squares (Q3a, Q10a, Q11a)
  - Five - 1 3/4" x 2 3/4" (A16, B16)
- One 4 1/8" x 42" strip. From this, cut:
  - Five - 4 1/8" squares (A9, B9)

▢ **From Fabric III, cut: (dark olive print)**
- Two 2 7/8" x 42" strips. From these, cut:
  - One - 2 7/8" x 8 1/2" (Q9)
  - Two - 2 7/8" x 8 1/8" (E4, F4)
  - One - 2 7/8" x 5 3/4" (Q4)
  - Six - 2 7/8" squares (C1a, D1a, C2b, D2b, Q8a)
  - Two - 2 1/8" x 2 7/8" (Q7)
  - Two - 1 5/8" x 2 7/8" (C2a, D2a)
  - One - 1 3/4" square (Q6)
  - Three - 1 5/8" squares (C1b, D1b, Q4b)
  - One - 1 5/8" x 1 3/4" (Q5)

▢ **From Fabric IV, cut: (medium olive print)**
- One 4 1/4" x 42" strip. From this, cut:
  - Five - 4 1/4" squares (A8, B8)
  - Two - 1 3/4" x 2 7/8" (C2a, D2a) stack this cut

* Eight - 1 3/4" squares (A12, B12, E3, F3, Q6) stack this cut

**From Fabric V, cut: (bright lime green print)**
• One 2 7/8" x 42" strip. From this, cut:
    * Five - 2 7/8" squares (C1, D1, E1a, F1a, Q4a)
    * Five - 2 1/4" x 2 7/8" (A11, B11)

**From Fabric VI, cut: (light olive print)**
• Four 1 1/2" x 42" strips. From these, cut:
    * Five - 1 1/2" x 12 3/8" (A7, B7)
    * Five - 1 1/2" x 10 5/8" (A6, B6)
    * Five - 1 1/8" squares (A11c, B11c)

**From Fabric VII, cut: (bright yellow print)**
• One 1 3/4" x 42" strip. From this, cut:
    * Five - 1 3/4" x 4 5/8" (A4, B4)

**From Fabric VIII, cut: (rust print)**
• Five 2 1/2" x 42" strips for straight-grain binding
• Six 2" x 42" strips. From these, cut:
    * Four - 2" x 32 1/2" (Q12) Piece two together to make 64 1/2" length.
    * Two - 2" x 22 7/8" (Q13)

**From Fabric IX, cut: (bright gold print)**
• Five 12 1/2" squares for napkins.

**From Fabric X, cut: (gold stripe)**
• Five 12 1/2" squares for napkins.

**From Fabric XI, cut: (assorted colors of red, orange, yellow, rust and brown)**
• Fifteen 2 1/4" squares (A3, B3) cut in half diagonally
• 100 - 1 7/8" squares for corn. (A2, B2)

# ASSEMBLY

**Making Corn Blocks A and B**
**1.** Use diagonal corner technique to make five each of mirror image Unit 6, 8, 8a, 9, 9a, and 11.
**2.** Use diagonal end technique to make five of mirror image Unit 7. Refer to the diagrams at right for making the corn pockets. Follow the instructions and illustrations to make the corn pockets. As the diagrams are for Block A, refer to the block drawings for

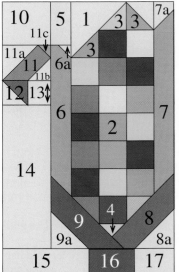

Block A, Make 3     Block B, Make 2

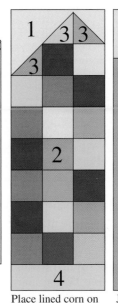

Lay corn right sides together on top of lining fabric. Using the corn as a pattern, cut the lining. Stitch across top as shown, trim tip and turn lining to back. Press.

Place lined corn on top of background, Unit A1 so that bottom raw edges are even. Pin in place. Join Unit 4, catching in the lined corn and the background.

Join units 6 and 7 to sides as shown, catching sides of pocket into seam.

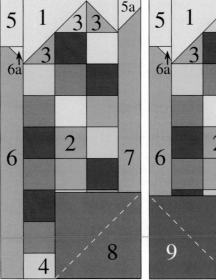
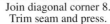

Join diagonal corner 8. Trim seam and press.

Join remainder of diagonal corners in alphabetical order.

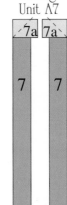

Making Unit A7

correct placement of mirror image units for Block B.
**3.** The drawing at left shows correct placement for making diagonal end Unit 7.
**4.** The gold box and diagrams on page 92 show the triangle-square technique used for Unit A12. Follow the instructions and drawings to make Unit 12.
**5.** To assemble the blocks, join units 12 and 13, referring frequently to block drawings at left for correct placement of mirror image units. Join units 10, 11, combined units 12-13 and Unit 14 in a vertical row. Add this row to the corn pocket. Join units 15, 16, and 17 in a horizontal row and join to bottom of blocks, matching seams.
**6.** Make three of Block A, and two of Block B.

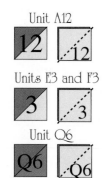

Unit A12

Units E3 and F3

Unit Q6

Use this assembly for Block A, Unit 12, Block E and F, Unit 3, and Unit Q6.
**1.** For Block A place 1 3/4" squares of fabrics I and IV right sides together, matching raw edges, and stitch a diagonal line down the center as shown. Press open and trim center seam, leaving the top and base fabric.
**2.** For blocks E and F, use 1 3/4" squares of fabrics I and IV.
**3.** For Unit Q6, use 1 3/4" squares of fabrics III and IV.

## Making Blocks C and D

1. Use diagonal corner technique to make one of mirror image Unit 1 for both blocks. To make Unit 2, refer to the diagram below and join a 1 5/8" x 2 7/8" strip of Fabric III with a 1 3/4" x 2 7/8" strip of Fabric IV, forming a square. This square is now used as a diagonal corner. Place it right sides together on Unit 2 as shown below. Stitch the diagonal, trim the center seam and press the corner up. To complete the unit, join 2b diagonal corner as shown.

2. To assemble the blocks, join Unit 1 to top of Unit 2, matching seams. Make one of each mirror image block.

Block C, Make 1   Block D, Make 1

Making Units C and D2

## Making Blocks E and F

1. Use diagonal corner technique to make two of mirror image Unit 1.
2, Use diagonal end technique to make two of mirror image Unit 4. Refer to diagram below for correct placement of the units.
3. Refer to the drawings and instructions in the gold box above for making Unit 3.
4. To assemble the block, join units 2 and 3, referring to block diagrams for correct placement of all mirror image units. Join Unit 1 to top of combined units 2-3; then add Unit 4 to the bottom to complete the blocks. Make one of Block E, and one of Block F.

## Assembling The Table Runner

1. Refer to the table runner drawing on page 92. Use diagonal corner technique to make one each of units Q3, Q4, Q8, Q10, and Q11.
2. Refer to the gold box at the top of page 92 for making Unit Q6 triangle-square. Follow the instructions given.
3. To assemble the table runner, begin at top right for row 1. Join one Block A, Unit Q3, another Block A, Unit Q11, and one Block B turned in the opposite direction. Match seams carefully when joining the blocks and "Q" units together.
4. For the center section, join units Q5 and Q6. Begin at the top of the row and join Block E, Block C, Unit 4, combine units 5-6, Unit 7, Unit 8, Unit 9, Block D, and Block F in a long vertical row. Join this row to row 1. Pin carefully to match all seams. Join Unit Q1 to top and bottom of the combined rows.
5. For row 3, join Unit Q2, Block B, Unit Q10, Block A (turned in the opposite direction, and Unit Q2. Join this row to the other two rows, matching seams.

Block E, Make 1   Block F, Make 1

Making Units E and F4

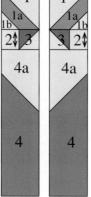
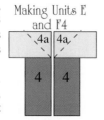

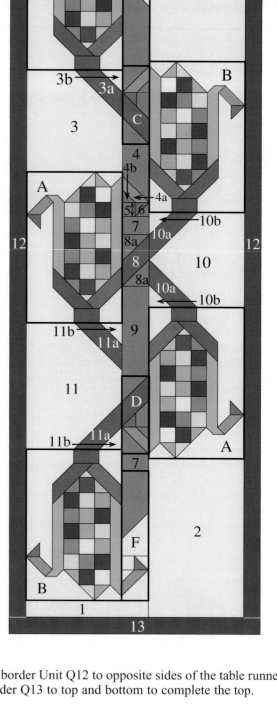

6. Join border Unit Q12 to opposite sides of the table runner; then add border Q13 to top and bottom to complete the top.

## Finishing

1. Faye found a lovely wheat stencil for this table runner. It was perfect with the background fabric (which had wheat on it) along with the border fabric that also had wheat on it. The patchwork was "ditched."
2. Use the 2 1/2" wide strips of Fabric VIII to make straight-grain french fold binding, and bind the table runner.
3. Refer to page 11 for instructions on making the reversible napkins. Fold the napkins as shown on page 11; then accordion fold them and place them in the corn pockets for the corn silk.

# Bloom Appétit

BLOOM APPETIT PLACE MAT.
Finishes to 14" x 18".
TABLE RUNNER Finishes to: 12" x 43".
CENTER PIECE Finishes to 20" circle.

### Pam's Chicken Salad With The Secret Ingredient.

#### Ingredients
1 cup diced celery
1 - 7 oz. jar of green olives with pimientos, sliced
1 cup chopped onion
1/3 cup sweet pickle relish
1/2 cup maraschino cherries, chopped
1/2 cup fresh blueberries
8 cups cooked boneless/skinless chicken
1 tsp. salt
1 tsp. seasoned pepper
1/4 tsp. crushed dill
1 tablespoon maraschino cherry juice
1 tablespoon Durkee's sauce
1 cup mayonnaise

#### Instructions
Combine first seven ingredients in a large bowl. Toss thoroughly. Add seasonings and toss into mixture. Add cherry juice, Durkee's and mayonnaise. Fold into other ingredients, mixing well.

Serve on tomato wedges.

## MATERIALS FOR TWO PLACE MATS

| | | |
|---|---|---|
| Fabric I (terra cotta print) Need 8 1/2" 3/8 yard | | |
| Fabric II (navy check) scrap | Need 7" x 9 1/2" | |
| Fabric III (bright yellow print) scrap | Need 6 1/2" x 8 1/2" | |
| Fabric IV (medium blue print) scrap | Need 4" x 8" | |
| Fabric V (medium green print) 1/4 yard | Need 6 3/4" | |
| Fabric VI (light blue sky print) 3/8 yard | Need 11 3/4" | |
| Fabric VII (bright gold print) scrap | Need 2 1/2" x 4 1/2" | |
| Fabric VIII (dark gray print) scrap | Need 4 1/4" x 7 1/2" | |
| Fabric IX (light gray print) scrap | Need 6 1/2" x 7 1/4" | |
| Fabric X (solid black) scrap | Need 1 3/4" x 7" | |
| Fabric XI (dark green print) 1 1/4 yard | Need 39" | |
| Fabric XII (light green print) 1/2 yard. | Need 12 1/2" | |
| 18" wide Steam-A-Seam 2 | 3/4 yard | |
| Backing Need 14" x 18" for each place mat. | | |
| Tear-away stabilizer | 1/2 yard | |

Be creative with your next patio picnic! Serve some potato chips in a new clay flower pot!

When you accidentally break a cup or saucer from a cute set that you just adored, don't toss the others or sell them at a yard sale. Use them as starter pots for small plants so that they can be displayed with the greenery!

94

## CUTTING FOR TWO PLACE MATS

*\* We have calculated the amount of fabric needed for the appliqué's, and the pieces to be cut from the fabric size given are indicated with each cut. Appliqué pattern pieces are found on large pattern sheet.*

**From Fabric I, cut: (terra cotta print)**
• Four 8 1/2" squares to cut flower pots and linings.

**From Fabric II, cut: (navy check)**
• One 7" x 9 1/2" for two flower pot bands #2, two small flower centers #6, two large flowers, and two large flower centers.

**From Fabric III, cut: (bright yellow print)**
• One 6 1/2" x 8 1/2" for four of flower #3, two large flowers, and four large flower centers.

**From Fabric IV, cut: (medium blue print)**
• One 4" x 8" for two large flowers, and four of small flower centers #4.

**From Fabric V, cut: (medium green print)**
• One 2 3/4" x 42" strip. From this, cut:
  * Two - 2 3/4" x 18" (grass, pieced)
• One 4"x 15" for twelve leaves.

**From Fabric VI, cut: (light blue sky print)**
• One 11 3/4" x 42" strip. From this, cut:
  * Two - 11 3/4" x 18" (sky, pieced)

**From Fabric VII, cut: (bright gold print)**
• One 2 1/2" x 4 1/2" for two small flowers #5.

**From Fabric VIII, cut: (dark gray print)**
• One 4 1/4" x 7 1/2" for two trowel units 7 and 9.

**From Fabric IX, cut: (light gray print)**
• One 6 1/2" x 7 1/4" for two trowel tops, Unit 8.

**From Fabric X, cut: (solid black)**
• One 1 3/4" x 7" for two trowel handles, Unit 10.

**From Fabric XI, cut: (dark green print)**
• Two 12 1/2" squares for napkins.
• Four 3 1/2" x 42" strips for binding.

**From Fabric XII, cut: (light green print)**
• Two 12 1/2" squares for napkins.

## ASSEMBLY

With napkin.    Behind napkin.

**1.** Our appliqué patterns are all numbered, and appliqué's should be pressed in place in numerical order. Refer to the large pattern sheet for the patterns and instructions for cutting. Refer to page 8

for making the binding frame, and page 11 for appliqué directions.

**2.** Cut the flower pot for the place mats on the solid line of the pattern. Place the flower pot fabric, and lining fabric right sides together and cut out. Stitch together on the seam line, leaving an opening to turn. Turn right side out and close with a piece of Steam-A-Seam 2.

**3.** Join the 2 3/4" x 18" piece of Fabric V to the 11 3/4" x 42" piece of fabric VI. This is your background. Sandwich batting between backing and top, and make the binding frame. Lined flower pot will be placed first. Top stitch around 3 sides of the pot, leaving the top open, forming the pocket. The pot will overlap the binding frame on the left. Continue pressing the appliqués in place and satin stitch around them to complete the place mat.

**4.** Refer to page 11 for reversible napkins. Appliqué a flower on both sides of the napkin. Stitch right sides together as directed on page 11.

## MATERIALS FOR TABLE RUNNER

| | | |
|---|---|---|
| Fabric I (terra cotta print) 3/8 yard | Need 8 1/2" |
| Fabric II (navy check) scrap | Need 10" x 18" |
| Fabric III (bright yellow print) scrap | Need 8" x 18" |
| Fabric IV (medium blue print) 3/8 yard | Need 8 1/2" |
| Fabric V (medium green print) 3/8 yard | Need 10" |
| Fabric VI (bright gold print) scrap | Need 2 1/4" x 10 1/2" |
| Fabric VII (dark green print) 3/4 yard | Need 25" |
| Fabric VIII (light green print) 3/4 yard | Need 25" |
| Fabric IX (dark brown print) 5/8 yard | Need 20 1/2" |
| 18" wide Steam-A-Seam 2 | 3/4 yard |
| Tear-away stabilizer | 1 yard |
| Backing | 1/2 yard |

## CUTTING

**From Fabric I, cut: (terra cotta print)**
• One 8 1/2" x 39" for flower box center

**From Fabric II, cut: (navy check)**
• One 10" x 18" for five flower pot bands #2, five large flowers, five large flower centers and ten small flower centers # 4.

**From Fabric III, cut: (bright yellow print)**
• One 8" x 18" for five large flowers, 10 small flowers #3, and five large flower centers.

**From Fabric IV, cut: (medium blue print)**
• One 8 1/2" x 23" for three pot tops, and 2 pot bottoms. Cut an extra 1 1/2" square for five small flower centers.

**From Fabric V, cut: (medium green print)**
• One 10" x 19" for three pot bottoms and two pot tops.
• One 5" x 18" for twenty leaves.

**From Fabric VI, cut: (bright gold print)**
• One 2 1/4" x 10 1/2" for five small flowers #5.

**From Fabric VII, cut: (dark green print)**
• Two 12 1/2" x 42" strips. From these, cut:
   * Five - 12 1/2" squares for napkins.

**From Fabric VIII, cut: (light green print)**
• Two 12 1/2" x 42" strips. From these, cut:
   * Five - 12 1/2" squares for napkins.

**From Fabric IX, cut: (dark brown print)**
• One 8 1/2" x 42 1/2" strip. From this, cut:
   * Five - 8 1/2" squares for flower pot linings.
• Three 2 1/2" x 42" strips for binding.
• One 2 1/4" x 43" strip for flower box top.
• One 2 1/4" x 39" strip for flower box bottom.

Trim corners on 45° angle    Right sides together

Right sides together

# ASSEMBLY

**1.** The table runner is a flower box with the pots sitting in it. Napkins are placed in the pots along with forks and spoons for a buffet line.

**2.** To make the flower box, join the Fabric IX top and bottom to the top and bottom of the Fabric I flower box center as shown above. Trim the 45° angle on the top as directed.

**3.** We placed the batting and backing behind the flower box, trimmed it to match and bound the entire flower box before adding the pots. This gave it stability. Be sure to pin or baste the 3 layers together.

**4.** The flower pots are found on the large pattern sheet with directions for cutting the different colors. Cut the flower pots as instructed on the large pattern sheet. Fuse the flower pot together before lining it. Press the band and small flowers onto the flower pots; then join the lining along the top seam, right sides together. Stitch across the top and press lining to inside. Place tear-away stabilizer behind the pot, and satin stitch the band and flowers in place.

**5.** Place strips of Steam-A-Seam 2 along all inside edges of the flower pots, except across the top. Refer to photo of the table runner and press the flower pots (staggered) as shown. Begin 1/4" from each end. Pin or baste the flower pots in place, and satin stitch them around the three sides, stitching through all layers. Tops are left open forming the pocket.

**6.** Refer to Step 4 in making the place mats to assemble the napkins.

## MATERIALS FOR CENTER PIECE

Fabric I (terra cotta print)    Need 9 1/4"
   3/8 yard
Fabric II (navy check)    Need 20"
   5/8 yard
Fabric III (medium green print)    Need 8 1/2"
   3/8 yard
Fabric IV (bright yellow print)    Need 7 1/4" x 8 1/2"
   scrap
Fabric V (medium blue print)    Need 7 1/4" x 8 1/2"
   scrap
18" wide Steam-A-Seam 2    1/2 yard
Tear

# CUTTING

**From Fabric I, cut: (terra cotta print)**
• One 9 1/4" circle.

**From Fabric II, cut: (navy check)**
• One 20' circle, and one 18" square to cut 2 1/2" strips for 70" of bias binding.

**From Fabric III, cut: (medium green print)**
• One 8 1/2" circle.
• One 3 1/2" x 15 1/2" for sixteen leaves.

**From Fabric IV, cut: (bright yellow print)**
• One 7 1/4" x 8 1/2" for four large flowers and four large flower centers.

**From Fabric V, cut: (medium blue print)**
• One 7 1/4" x 8 1/2" for four large flowers and four large flower centers.

# ASSEMBLY

**1.** Begin with your backing and batting, which needs to be cut to a 22" circle. Center the 20" circle of Fabric II on the batting. Pin all layers together.

**2.** Press Steam-A-Seam 2 to the back of the remaining circles. Find the center of the 20" circle, and center the 9 1/4" circle of Fabric I on the 20" circle. Press it in place. Center the 8 1/2" circle of Fabric III on the 9 1/4" circle and press in place. Satin stitch around the two center circles through all thicknesses. Press.

**3.** Using a water erasable pen, find the center of the circle, and draw placement lines through the circle, vertically and horizontally. Draw two 45° lines, dissecting the circle into eights. Place the

flowers centered on the lines and press them in place.

**4.** Satin stitch the flowers and leaves through all thicknesses. Satin stitch the stems in green.

**5.** Cut and join 70" of 2 1/2" wide bias binding from Fabric II. Trim backing and batting to match circle top and bind the center piece.

**6.** Use as a place to put a bowl for serving or a plant for decoration.